GROOVY MOVIES

Other titles in The Knowledge series:

GROOVY MOVIES

MARTIN OLIVER

ILLUSTRATED BY TONY REEVE

For Katie – the grooviest mover I know

Scholastic Children's Books,
Commonwealth House, 1-19 New Oxford Street,
London WC1A 1NU, UK

A division of Scholastic Limited
London ~ New York ~ Toronto ~ Sydney ~ Auckland

Published in the UK by Scholastic Ltd, 1998
Text copyright © Martin Oliver, 1998
Illustrations copyright © Tony Reeve, 1998

ISBN: 0 590 19018 0

Typeset by TW Typesetting, Midsomer Norton, Avon
Printed and bound by Nørhaven Paperback, Viborg, Denmark

10

The right of Martin Oliver and Tony Reeve to be identified
as the author and illustrator of this work respectively has been
asserted by them in accordance with the Copyright, Designs and
Patents Act, 1988.

Contents

CONTENTS

INTRODUCTION

Almost everyone thinks that movies are groovy. Even parents have a favourite film or movie star. You could try and ask your mum and dad who they like, but be prepared, they may get carried away.

Movies arrived a long time ago. They've been around for over a hundred years, and fantastic new ones are being made all the time.

So why are films so funky? Is it because:
● being a movie star is the grooviest job going
● you think that animation is awesome
● film fashion is fabulous
● you want to get in on the action and become a dynamic director

If you think it's one or all of them, then you're beginning to get the picture. It's not just what's on the silver screen that's groovy, it's what goes on behind it too. Ever since pictures began moving, the big screen has attracted larger than life characters and larger than life incidents.

Alfred Hitchcock said that: and he's right, there's hardly ever a dull moment in the movie world. So, if you want to find out about marauding movie moguls, how to become a superstar and even test your friends with our Movie Buff-buster Quizzes, then turn up the lights, and turn off your camera for the *grooviest* movie action.

> FILM IS LIFE WITH ALL THE BORING BITS TAKEN AWAY

GROOVY MOVIE TIMELINE

1535 Italian boffin Girolamo Cardano fixes a lens into a hole in the wall of a darkened room. The lens projects an upside down image of the view outside the room. He names this early projector a "camera obscura" meaning "dark room", rather than the more accurate "dark room with a hole knocked in it".

1700 Shadow shows in Java use complicated puppets to make the first moving pictures (Simpler versions existed in China in 121 BC.). Narrators tell the story while orchestras provide sound effects.

1765 Frenchman Chevalier D'Arcy demonstrates his "Persistence of Vision" theory by attaching a hot coal to the end of a rope and spinning it round in a darkened room. His theory – that the image of the moving object remains for a fraction of a second after the object has gone – is correct, but amazingly he is ignored for about fifty years. Well, you try ignoring someone whirling hot coals around their head.

1798 Belgian showman, Etienne Robertson, terrifies audiences with his Phantasmagoria. Held in theatres decorated to look like Gothic ruins, he uses a modified magic lantern[1] to make skeletons hover over viewers' heads.

1827 One summer morning, Nicephore Niepce, begins setting up his photographic equipment – a camera obscura lens and a plate of light-sensitive chemicals. Eight hours later, the

[1]Early magic lanterns used a candle, a lens and painted strips of glass to project pictures. Later on, the candle was replaced with a gas light. This produced brighter pictures but gas was unreliable and sometimes produced unexpected special effects.

exposure is complete and the world's first still photograph has been taken.

1872 American railway tycoon Leland Stanford bets $25,000 that a horse lifts all its hooves off the ground when galloping. He hires photographer Eadweard Muybridge to prove him right. Six years later, Muybridge invents a camera shutter that opens and closes fast enough to film a horse's hooves and he is able to take a sequence of photographs that win the bet.

1885 George Eastman has the bright idea of coating rolls of paper with light-sensitive chemicals and invents the first photographic film. He adds sprockets to advance his reels and loads them into his Kodak camera.

1888 The very first motion pictures, showing traffic moving over a bridge in Leeds, are taken by Louis Le Prince. Le Prince spends two years modifying his

moving picture camera until he is ready to display his invention abroad. In a mystery worthy of a Hollywood thriller, he boards the Dijon-Paris train but never arrives in Paris. No trace of his body is ever found and the mystery of his disappearance has never been solved.

1889 Thomas Edison's assistant, William Dickson, perfects a movie camera. He and Edison make a short film of a man who bows, smiles and takes off his hat. Edison claims the credit and the copyright for the invention which he calls the Kinetograph.

1895 French brothers, Auguste and Louis Lumiere, patent the Cinematographe[2] which is a combined camera and projector operating at sixteen frames a second. The brothers then put on the first paying film show in a basement of a Parisian café

[2]The Cinematographe was based on the design of a sewing machine. It was so successful that the Lumières soon had the film market stitched up.

and encounter a problem – only thirty-five people turn up. But the news gets round and within weeks thousands of people are queuing outside and this leads to another problem – the brothers need a bigger basement.

1896 Queen Victoria becomes the first British Monarch to be filmed during her autumn holiday at Balmoral. Her reaction is not known.

1898 Film maker George Méliès' camera jams. When it begins working again, Méliès sees that the bus he was filming has changed into a hearse. The special effects industry is born.

1904 The first children's cinema show is held in Derbyshire. This sounds like a good thing. Unfortunately, it is run by teachers who promise that their films will be "quite free from vulgarity throughout". The audience soon decide this is a bad thing and the shows stop.

1907 Movie-makers begin to move to a sleepy town on the west coast of America called Hollywood. In the first film explosion, the population grows from under 5,000 to 130,000 by 1925.

1913 Italian movie *Quo Vadis* hits the screen, lasting for over two hours. Movie makers are amazed that audiences manage to sit throughout the entire film which becomes the first feature-length movie.

1914 A little-known actor called Charlie Chaplin creates "the little tramp" character. Within two years, he becomes the highest-paid film star in the world with a yearly salary of $670,000 – the richest little tramp in the world.

1927 *The Jazz Singer*, starring Al Jolson, is released. This becomes known as the first talkie although only 354 words are spoken in it. Within three years, all feature films become talkies – a case of silent movies going quietly.

1931 After two years handing out "The Statuettes" at The Academy Awards Ceremony, the Academy's librarian, Margaret Herrick, remarks that they look like her Uncle Oscar. The name sticks and the awards become known as the Oscars.

1935 The first full-length Technicolor film arrives. *Becky Sharp* (a historical drama based on Thackeray's *Vanity Fair*) is not a complete success. One critic describes the actors as looking like "boiled salmon dipped in mayonnaise…"

1951 The number of television sets in America rockets from 6,500 at the end of the war to over 11,000,000. Movie makers get ready to battle against "the little monster in the living room".

1952 Cinerama is unveiled by film bosses who decide that big is best. Unfortunately, they soon discover that huge pictures mean huge costs. Eventually Cinerama goes the same way as Cinemascope,

Vistavision and SuperScope. Round 1 to television.

1977 *Star Wars* wins seven Oscars for special effects. Its success resurrects the special effects industry where computers are used for the first time.

1979 After 50 years of showing news reels in cinemas, the last MovieTone News is broadcast in Britain. Its final pictures show the Chelsea Flower Show, aerial pictures of London and highlights of the past half century.

1982 A film featuring a character who looks like a mixture of Albert Einstein and a newborn baby becomes a huge hit. *E.T. – The Extra-Terrestrial* takes $700 million worldwide.

1990 The Indian film industry makes a world record 948 full-length feature films this year. Based in Bombay, Bollywood regularly releases more feature films than Hollywood.

1993 *Jurassic Park* breaks box office records when it becomes one of the most successful films ever. The monster success of the film is ensured by a $68 million publicity budget which is $8 million more than the cost of actually making the film and enough to buy a T-Rex sized amount of publicity. The film also breaks new ground by containing over five minutes of computer generated animation.

1996 *Toy Story* becomes the first feature film to be entirely computer generated. While its characters may only exist in virtual reality, its profits are absolutely real.

GROOVY MOVIE GOOFS AND GAFFES

Old goofs...

When movies first appeared, audiences thought that they were a miracle, but it wasn't a miracle that happened overnight. Making pictures move turned out to be even more difficult than doing a chemistry test. You might think that things would have gone smoothly for early inventors but their huge brain-power didn't stop them making some groovy goofs. In fact, they made so many mistakes that it's a miracle that pictures ever moved at all.

1 Belgian scientist, Joseph Plateau, who lived from 1801 to 1883, had already made one ghastly gaffe when he damaged his eyes from studying the sun through a telescope. Undeterred by this slight inconvenience, he continued working and in the 1830s he was putting the finishing touches to his latest invention. It was simple enough to use:

Take disc with images painted on it and attach it to handle.

Spin the disc.

Observe spinning disc in a mirror where the images appear to move.

But it wasn't so easy to pronounce the name of Plateau's invention – The Phenakistoscope.

Eventually, the barmy Belgian realized that this unpronounceable name might have been a goof and he renamed his device the Fantascope, but its novelty soon wore off and sales plummeted.

2 Eadweard Muybridge's development of the camera shutter in 1872 was a remarkable achievement but it was even more remarkable that Muybridge was alive to make it. A few years earlier, he had made a gruesome goof by killing his wife's boy-friend. Luckily for him, and for movies, he was let off by the judge and was able to continue with his experiments.

3 All-round egg-head and inventor extraordinaire, Thomas Edison, designed a moving picture camera called the Kinetograph. The camera was a success and films shot with the Kinetograph were shown in Kinetoscope parlours all around the world but there was a design drawback – only one person could view each film at a time!

KINETOSCOPE PARLOUR

HOUSE FULL

4 The Lumière Brothers' Cinematographe machine solved this problem and was able to show films to large audiences but the brothers didn't seem to realize quite what they had done. Their father told a film fan that "this invention ... can be exploited for a while as a scientific curiosity: beyond that it has no commercial value." After a few years the Lumières stopped making movies, leaving others to earn fortunes from films instead.

5 Within a few years of their invention, moving pictures set the whole world alight – in some cases, literally. When George Eastman had made films by coating paper with light-sensitive chemicals, he overlooked the fact that these chemicals were highly flammable. This proved to be a grisly gaffe. In May 1897, films caught fire at a moving picture show at the Paris Charity Bazaar, and the inferno that followed killed over a hundred people from France's most aristocratic families. Years later, another goof came to light when it was discovered that these chemicals were also unstable and they were destroying the film reels.

6 The arrival of talkies in 1927 led to a new batch of technological goofs. Pallophotophone,

Madalatone, Synchroscope and Phonocinematoph were all sound systems with impressive-sounding names that sounded less than impressive in cinemas.

The Vitaphone system which was used with *The Jazz Singer* in 1927 was supposed to synchronize the movie sound track with the on-screen action but it would often slip out of synch so that speeches did not match up with the actor who was speaking on the screen. After two years and too many slip-ups (or slip-outs) the plug was pulled on Vitaphone and it was replaced with the new Movietone sound-on film process.

New gaffes

Those great film pioneers weren't the only people to make mistakes. Even when the technology of moving pictures was up and running smoothly, there was a whole new group of movie people ready to make groovy goofs:

1 In 1898, the producers of *The Passion Play*, thought it would be a good idea to hire the famous stage director, L.J. Vincent, to be the very first film

director. Unfortunately, the appointment of Mr Vincent turned out to be gigantic goof. He had never seen a movie in his life and didn't understand the idea of moving pictures. The dreadful director was convinced that the camera could only take still photographs so whenever the actors began moving, he would yell "hold it". The film was only made because of a crafty cameraman called William Paley. After a few

useless hours with Mr Vincent in charge, the cameraman would tell the director that there wasn't enough light to continue filming. The actors and crew would then pretend to pack up while the director left. As soon as the disastrous director had gone, the cast and crew would sneak back onto the set and film as much as possible. The ruse worked and the film was a sensation when it was eventually completed.

2 An open-air cinema might sound like a good idea, but putting it in the north of England was not quite so clever. The Garden Cinema opened in Hull in July 1912. Customers sat on deckchairs in an open-sided marquee. It closed when winter arrived and *stayed* closed.

3 The bigger you are in the movie world, the bigger mistakes you can make and movie moguls didn't come much bigger than Louis B. Meyer, head of the massive MGM studio. In 1928, he viewed a film by an unknown film-maker but refused to give the young man a contract because he thought that pregnant women would be frightened of a ten-foot tall rodent on the screen. The film-maker was Walt Disney and the rodent was Mickey Mouse.

4 Meyer's head of production, Irving Thalberg, made two equally ghastly gaffes. He dismissed the success of *The Jazz Singer* (1927) with the confident prediction that "talking pictures are just a passing phase" and some years later, he advised his boss to stay clear of *Gone with the Wind* with the comment that "no Civil War picture ever made a nickel".

As we now know, talking pictures have been a passing phase that has lasted over *seventy* years and *Gone with the Wind* is one of the most famous movies ever made.

5 Screen superstars have made some crazy mistakes too. In the classic comedy, *Big Business*, viewers watch Laurel and Hardy wreck a bungalow. Unfortunately, they destroyed the wrong one. They picked a bungalow owned by a studio employee and promised to rebuild it when they had finished filming, but they got the wrong address. They only realized their goof when the bungalow's owners arrived in the middle of filming to find that their home had been destroyed.

6 Douglas Fairbank's 1922 version of *Robin Hood* scored a bullseye – in more ways than one. When he was publicising the film on the roof of the Ritz Hotel in New York, Fairbanks got so carried away that he fired off an arrow by mistake. It flew through the air, hitting a tailor on the bottom. The unfortunate man thought that he was being attacked by Native Americans. It took a well-publicised hospital visit from the movie star and a less well-publicised $5,000 payoff to put right the ghastly goof.

...AND AN EXTRA $10 FOR MENDING THE TROUSERS!

7 Tom Selleck was all set to play the lead in a major blockbuster film when he discovered that he could not get out of a commitment to a television programme called *Magnum P.I.* His gaffe cost him the chance to appear in the film. Harrison Ford got the part instead and became a mega star for his performance as Indiana Jones in *Raiders of the Lost Ark*.

Screen Test

Do you know someone who thinks they are a film buff? Does your dad reckon he knows more about movies than Barry Norman? Why not call his bluff and try him out on the:

1 What is the most expensive film ever made? Is it...?

   a *Terminator II*
   b *Waterworld*
   c *Titanic*

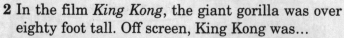

2 In the film *King Kong*, the giant gorilla was over eighty foot tall. Off screen, King Kong was...

   a a six foot actor in a gorilla suit
   b a 23 inch model
   c a seven foot ape

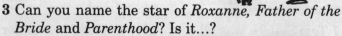

3 Can you name the star of *Roxanne, Father of the Bride* and *Parenthood*? Is it...?

   a Julia Roberts
   b Steve Martin
   c Macaulay Culkin

4 Most actors fade away at the end of their career but one went on to become the President of the United States? Was it...?

a Charles Chaplin
b Humphrey Bogart
c Ronald Reagan

5 Who played the part of the caped crusader in the 1994 film, *Batman Forever*? Was it...?

a Val Kilmer
b Michael Keaton
c Jack Nicholson

6 Hollywood hopeful Archibald Leach decided to change his name when he arrived in America (well, do *you* know any movie stars called Archibald?). What did he call himself?

a Harrison Ford
b Errol Flynn
c Cary Grant

7 Your dad may think he can do Tarzan's call, but does he know how it was originally made? Was it a combination of...?

a a yodeller and a man gargling water
b a camel's bleat, a hyena's howl and a plucked violin
c an opera singer's voice played backwards

8 Which of the following characters has appeared in the most films? Is it...?

a Sherlock Holmes

b Robin Hood

c Frankenstein's monster

9 Ian Fleming, the creator of *James Bond*, also wrote a children's film. Was it...?

a *Chitty Chitty Bang Bang*

b *Mrs Doubtfire*

c *101 Dalmatians*

10 When Western star, Clint Eastwood, was elected Sheriff, er, Mayor of Carmel, his first act was to...

a ban on-street parking

b license a 24 hour cinema

c legalise ice cream parlours

True or False

11 Mickey Mouse was originally called Mortimer Mouse.

12 Steven Spielberg had never won an Oscar before making *Schindler's List*.

13 Charlie Chaplin once entered a Chaplin look-alike contest – and came second.

14 Five different actors have played James Bond in the famous 007 series.

15 Fidel Castro, President of Cuba, once worked as a film extra in Hollywood.

Multiple choice answers

1-c Titanic's titanic budget of over $200 million swamped all previous records as well as swamping its cast who had to be tied down during the storm scene to stop them going overboard.

2-b The miniscule model of King Kong was covered with foam rubber and rabbit fur.

I LOVE IT BUT LOSE THE EARS

3-b Steve Martin. By the way, his grey hair is natural. It turned that colour when he was still a teenager.

4-c Ronald Reagan (President of the U.S. 1981–1989.) was a B movie star of the 40s and 50s. In his most popular film, *Bedtime for Bonzo*, he acted with a monkey – ideal training for a life in politics.

5-a When *Batman Returns* was released in North America in 1992, it was shown on a then record-breaking 3,700 screens.

6-c The name change worked and Cary Grant soon became a groovy movie idol. He starred in classic comedy *Bringing Up Baby* and Hitchcock's *North by Northwest* but he never won an Oscar.

7-b Cuddly Cheetah the chimpanzee who starred in the Tarzan movies didn't enjoy a happy retirement – he was sold to a circus.

SO WHERE'S MY DRESSING ROOM?

8-a Elementary, my dear Watson. Sherlock Holmes has appeared in 211 films, Robin Hood in 58 and Frankenstein's monster in 115.

9-a Ian Fleming actually worked for the British Intelligence Service. Maybe flying cars were one of the gadgets that British spies used.

10c Lawman Clint was quick on the draw to legalise ice-cream parlours. Later on, he was gunning for skateboarders when he outlawed skateboards from Carmel.

True or false answers

11 True – but Mickey wasn't Walt Disney's first animated hero. Walt started his animation career with a character called Oswald the Lucky Rabbit. When Oswald didn't prove to be very lucky, Disney went back to the drawing board to produce Mickey.

12 True. Until '94, Spielberg had won nothing despite directing *Jaws*, *E.T.* and *Jurassic Park*.

13 False. Chaplin did enter a look-alike contest but he came third!

14 True. They are: Sean Connery, George Lazenby, Roger Moore, Timothy Dalton and Pierce Brosnan.

15 True. No other movie extras have become presidents but Marlene Dietrich, Clark Gable and Marilyn Monroe were all extras who became stars.

GROOVY STARS

When it comes to funky film jobs, what could be groovier than being a movie star? Who wouldn't like the fame and the admiration of thousands of fans – not to mention a few million dollars thrown in? Nowadays, Sylvester Stallone and Arnold Schwarzenegger are some of the most famous people in the world. These mega-stars expect very special treatment but there was a time when things were very different. If an actor got a break in an early movie, they soon discovered that they were not top of the bill when it came to filming.

For the first ten years of film making, there were no stars at all. Cameras were the most important things on set and if there were any signs of bad weather, the camera was immediately sheltered, not the actors.

Horses were considered much more valuable than human actors too, and were better treated. After all, you could always get another actor but trained horses were much harder to find!

In the beginning, actors went along with this. They didn't want their names known because working in movies was seen as a sign that they had failed at acting in the theatre. The film companies were quite happy too – not having stars meant that they could pay all their actors the same.

Things only changed in 1910, when an American film producer, Carl Laemmle, lured away the most popular actress from a rival studio. He then dreamt up a huge publicity campaign in which the actress's name was revealed as Florence Lawrence. Laemmle's plan worked perfectly. Within a year, Florence Lawrence had become a star and her name was being printed above the title of the films she was in.

The star system soon spread throughout the world but along with star performances, came star egos and temper tantrums. In the same year that Florence Lawrence shot to stardom, the name of a German actress, Henny Porten, appeared on the credits of a successful film. The new German star immediately insisted on a 10% salary increase for appearing in her next movie. The film producer refused but was forced to give in when she threatened to walk off the set.

Two years later, the first superstar salary arrived. The lucky star was a Danish actress called Asta Nielson. She was guaranteed annual pay of $80,000 while Florence Lawrence's pay in the same year was a trifling $13,000. On that sort of money, poor old Florence would have found that after buying a large house, she'd only have enough change for a pair of Rolls Royces!

Star spotting

Unless you're lucky enough to live in Beverly Hills or get invited to movie premiers, film stars can be a bit thin on the ground. But, sometimes stars turn up in the unlikeliest places and star spotters should always looks out for those give-away signs.

Leading man

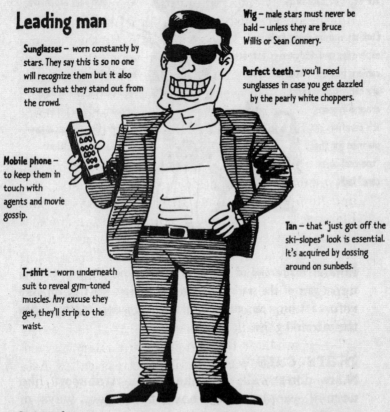

Sunglasses – worn constantly by stars. They say this is so no one will recognize them but it also ensures that they stand out from the crowd.

Wig – male stars must never be bald – unless they are Bruce Willis or Sean Connery.

Perfect teeth – you'll need sunglasses in case you get dazzled by the pearly white choppers.

Mobile phone – to keep them in touch with agents and movie gossip.

Tan – that "just got off the ski-slopes" look is essential. It's acquired by dossing around on sunbeds.

T-shirt – worn underneath suit to reveal gym-toned muscles. Any excuse they get, they'll strip to the waist.

Beware! Stars look smaller in real life than they do on screen and some of them are quite small to begin with – Michael J. Fox is 5 foot 4 in and Dustin Hoffman is 5 foot 5 in.

Leading lady

Improbably large chest – result of visit to various plastic surgeons. Also check behind ears of older stars for signs of face lifts.

Hair – always immaculate. Accompanied by make-up that took two hours to apply.

Perfect teeth – blinding white "Hollywood smile". Very bright and very expensive.

Clothes – mind-bogglingly expensive, and designed to attract camera flashes. If star actresses are caught mooching around in jeans, it's carefully planned for that "too cool to care" look.

Very thin – result of rigorous diets and daily sessions with a personal trainer. Oh, and occasional surgical intervention.

Beware! That crowd of people surrounding the star are not fans, they're part of the star's entourage. Movie stars won't go anywhere without a stylist, a personal assistant and a bodyguard – and that's when they're travelling light.

Stars' cars

Stars don't walk or take public transport like normal people. They have their own ways of travelling that can be a dead giveaway. In the past, it was fairly easy to spot some stars' cars: after the success of her 1927 film *It*, Clara Bow painted her convertible red to match her hair while Tom Mix, a cowboy star of the 1920s, had a saddle and steer horns on the bonnet.

Modern day stars aren't as conspicuous but committed star-spotters should keep their eyes peeled for:

Stretch limousine – the most popular form of star travel. The general rule being the bigger the car, the bigger the star. Clark Gable had his car customised so that it was exactly one foot longer than a rival's. It was rumoured that Cher once refused to attend a function unless she was transported in the longest stretch limo in the country.

Armoured car – one of Arnold Schwarzenegger's more unusual forms of transport is a Humvee armoured car donated to him by the American army.

Lear jet – costing $15 million apiece, owning one of these is the sign of truly groovy star status. Tom Cruise and John Travolta both pilot their own jets.

Star steps

How do people get to be stars in the first place? How did they turn their school play success into Hollywood heart-throb status? If you think that your killer comedy routine deserves more attention than it's getting at the moment then read the indispensable groovy movie guide – ten different ways to become a superstar.

1 **Start young.** Macaulay Culkin followed in the footsteps of other child actors such as Shirley Temple and Judy Garland (he appeared in *Home Alone II* at the grand old age of twelve). The problem with this method is that your film careers tends to be over before you finish school. Don't worry if you haven't made it by 16 though, Humphrey Bogart didn't star in a film until he was in his forties and Jessica Tandy was 80 years old when she won an Oscar for *Driving Miss Daisy*. So there's even hope for your parents if they want to get in on the movie act!

2 **Be related to someone in the movies.** There are lots of famous film families. Kirk Douglas's son, Michael is a major star. Charlie Sheen's dad is Martin Sheen and his cousin is Emilio Estevez. Drew Barrymore's relatives include a

34

silent movie star and a grandmother who played Jane in some of the Tarzan films. If you aren't lucky enough to be born into a film family, why not try the route taken by Nicole Kidman and Cindy Crawford and get hitched to a film star? Nicole married Tom Cruise and Cindy married Richard Gere.

3 Be persistent. Don't be put off by the discouraging things people say and never give up trying. Fred Astaire's screen test said "Can't act. Can't sing. Can dance a little." One movie hopeful's screen test for 20th Century Fox was such a a disaster that it was preserved and used as a classic example of how *not* to perform in front of the camera. Undeterred by this celluloid catastrophe, the actor went on to become the 50s and 60s movie idol, Rock Hudson.

When he was still an unknown actor, Michael Caine never gave up hope – even after one awesomely awful audition...

4 Change your name. Winona Horowitz and T.C. Mapother IV changed their careers when they changed their names to Winona Ryder and Tom Cruise. John Wayne might not have been so convincing as a tough guy if he'd kept his original name – Marion Morrison. One man who ignored this tip and made it to the top with an almost unpronounceable name is Arnold Schwarzenegger, but maybe no one dared suggest a name change!

5 Always say yes – the golden rule for anyone starting out in the movies. During auditions for a musical with an ice-skating scene, the entire group of extras told the producer they could ice skate. Six weeks later, once their costumes had been made and the ice rink built, the truth came out. Only four of them had been telling the truth. The other fifty-six could hardly stand up on the ice, let alone skate.

Mexican actor Antony Quinn was so desperate to act in films that when he was asked by the casting director if he could speak Cheyenne, he nodded his head and promptly spoke for two minutes in complete gibberish. Having fooled the director with his made-up Cheyenne, he was asked if he could ride a horse. He'd never been on a horse before but he quickly replied, "Oh sure, of course. Well ... not for a while, not, actually, since I left the reservation." He got the part and a free horse-riding "refresher" course.

6 **Win an Oscar.** This usually guarantees stardom, although it isn't the surefire success you might think. After all, big stars like Richard Burton and Peter Sellers never won Oscars and what about F. Murray Abraham? Exactly. He won the Best Actor Award in 1985 for *Amadeus* and no one has ever heard of him since.

7 **Be lucky.** Sickeningly enough, some people become stars without even meaning to! Bob Hoskins's acting career began purely by chance. He was waiting in a theatre bar to meet a friend who was auditioning for a part. The casting director spotted him and asked him to audition. He got a leading part and became a star – his friend didn't!

The story of silent star Florence Vidor's big break sounds like a corny movie plot.

In **Act 1**, the young girl is seen getting into the back seat of a car with her family. As they drive along, she is glimpsed by a handsome director.

In **Act 2**, the young director tracks down the girl to persuade her to act in his film but he runs into trouble in the shape of Florence's father who is outraged at the idea.

In **Act 3**, her father relents and allows his daughter to act in *The Tow*. Florence becomes a huge star but the story doesn't finish there. In true Hollywood style, there is an even happier ending. During filming, the director and his star fall in love, marry and live happily together.

After being told "you ain't got it, kid" by a movie mogul, Harrison Ford started up a successful carpentry business. He was working at night, installing a complicated panel in a film studio when he hit a problem and was forced to work the next day. It turned out to be the same day that George Lucas was casting for a new film and quicker than you can say *Star Wars*, Ford got the part of Han Solo and his superstar career was launched.

8 Be famous for doing something else first.
Johnny Weismuller was an Olympic swimming
champion before finding fame as Tarzan. Super-
model Cindy Crawford has just made her
feature film debut while Whitney Houston is the
latest in a long line of singers making it in the
movies. One of the biggest superstars (in every
way), Arnold Schwarzenegger, won the Mr
Universe body-building title seven times before
conquering the movie world.

WE'LL HAVE TO SHOOT
IN WIDESCREEN

9 Have some acting ability. This is an optional
extra, just ask Keanu Reeves – or "Keanu Act",
as he's known in Scotland.

KEANU'S ACTING CLASS:

1. LOVE   2. ANGER   3. JOY   4. FEAR

10 Early exit. Marilyn Monroe, James Dean and
River Phoenix have all guaranteed their superstar status by following this method and dying
young. The only drawback is that you're not
around to enjoy the benefits.

Star jobs

If your mum and dad have lumbered you with some grotty jobs around the house, don't worry, you're not alone. Even the biggest stars weren't born rich and famous and they too have had to do some dodgy or dreary jobs while waiting for their big break. See if you can match the job to the star in our mini:

a Sean Connery   **1** lion cage cleaner

b Geena Davis   **2** French polisher for a coffin maker

c Michelle Pfeiffer   **3** supermarket check-out cleaner

d Sylvester Stallone   **4** hotdog seller

e Sharon Stone   **5** living dummy for New York dress shop

CAN YOU INTRODUCE ME TO THE MGM LION?

Answers:
a2, b5, c3, d1, e4

Little big stars

You don't have to be big to be big in the movies. Movie makers are always looking for new child actors to add the "aaah" factor to their films, and some stars have become big long before they've even finished school. Being a child star sounds truly groovy. Just think, you wouldn't have to tidy your room or do the washing up.

So what's the catch? Well, unfortunately, all too often, the "aaah" factor can turn to the "aaargh" factor. Once you get that part in the latest Hollywood blockbuster, you may think your troubles are all over but they could just be starting. Happy endings on screen don't always guarantee happy endings in real life as child actors have discovered.

If you're not quite ready to book your one-way ticket to stardom, just sit back and play the movie game. All you do is throw a dice then follow the footprints on the yellow brick road. You'll find lots of detours and unexpected obstacles in the way but hopefully you'll just roll (or role) along until you reach the happy ending.

Your road to stardom board game

START: Congratulations. You've just arrived on the movie scene. Now you're all ready to follow the yellow brick road.

ROAD TO STARDOM

⑬

Cash bonanza. Money-bags Macaulay Caulkin has made more cash than any other child actor in history. In 1992, he took $5 million plus a percentage of profits from *Home Alone II: Lost in New York*.
Skip ahead five footprints to the bank.

⑩
Scare-cut. Shirley Temple was famous in the 1930s for her dimples and ringlets and for singing aboard *The Good Ship Lollipop*. When her ringlets were chopped off, her career wobbled for a while but later recovered.
Miss a go while your career is on ice.

③
Pushy parents. Judy Garland's parents put her on the stage with her two sisters at the age of six. At the age of 12, she was signed up for the MGM Studio.
Leap forward four footprints.

⑧
Cash catastrophe. Jackie Coogan was still at school when he signed a contract worth over $1 million. Unfortunately, his mother spent it all before he had left.
Go back to the start.

⑥
Amazing make-up. Seven-year-old Mickey Rooney's fair hair was darkened with shoe-polish and the new look actor landed the leading part in a series of comedy shorts.
Skip ahead two footprints.

19 **Dastardly director.** Directors have tried out some terrible tricks to get performances from child stars. When Shirley Temple had trouble crying on screen, directors lied to her, claiming that her pets had died. **Miss out a turn to dry your eyes.**

21 **Teenage terror.** Macaulay Culkin reached his teens and the film roles dried up. **Go back to bank and count your money while you wait for new parts.**

28 **Happy ending.** Congratulations, you've reached the end of the yellow brick road. If you're still in one piece, collect a round of applause.

18 **Award winner.** Margaret O'Brien won a special Academy Award as an "outstanding child actor" in 1944. She was seven years old. **Move forward five footprints.**

16 **Drug detour.** Drew Barrymore starred in *E.T. – The Extra Terrestrial* before she was ten. She later became a drug and alcohol addict – before she was fifteen. **Miss out two turns to recover** – like her, you'll probably get back in the movies later on.

24 **Dead end.** As a highly-strung child actor, Judy Garland was given pills to calm her down. Unfortunately, they made her sleepy so the studio gave her pills to wake up. Then, she couldn't sleep, so she was given even more pills. At the age of 57 she had taken so many pills that she couldn't wake up any more. **Drop out of the game.**

If you're hooked on the movie game, you might want to follow Jodie Foster into the sequel, Movie Game 2. Jodie Foster starred as a child actor in *Bugsy Malone* and is still acting. She won an Oscar in 1989 for *The Accused*, starred in the scary adult movie *Silence of the Lambs* and in the 1997 sci-fi movie, *Contact*.

Movie makeover

How keen would you be on getting into the movies? Some people will do almost anything to get themselves on screen but would you go as far as one Hollywood hopeful in the 1930s who went for a complete movie makeover...?

"I'm sorry kid, we're letting you go."

It was the moment that the young Spanish dancer had been dreading. Ever since Fox Films had been merged with 20th Century, there had been rumours about sackings. Margarita Cansino had been called into the producer's office, heart in her mouth.

"Pero Señor," she mumbled. "But Señor, I know how to sing and to dance."

"I've got a lot of girls who can do the same."

"Si, si, but I am learning. I go, er ... how you say it? I go drama school and speak classes."

"Sure, I know, you're a trier but what can I do? There aren't enough roles for Spanish dancers. I'm sorry. My hands are tied – we're letting your contract lapse."

Margarita tried to convince the producer that he was wrong but it was no good, she couldn't change his mind. Blinking back the tears, Margarita walked out of the studio and out of the movies. Somehow she found her way back to her apartment where she tried to think about what she should do now. Losing her job at the studio was a disaster. She couldn't imagine a life outside show business. She had been on stage since she was six, she didn't know anything else.

She thought back to the morning's meeting. What had that slimey producer said? That's it ... "you're a trier ... there aren't enough roles for Spanish dancers."

Well, he was right. She was a trier and if he expected her to just roll over and give up, he was wrong. Margarita clenched her fists. She was determined not to fail. She was going to get back into the movies, but how?

Over the next few weeks, she racked her brains. Most people would have given up hope, but not her. She knew that she had star quality. Still, unless she could get back in front of the camera, nobody would ever see what she had to offer. What could she do to change the studio's mind?

"Change … change … *change!*" The word echoed in Margarita's mind until an extraordinary thought came to her. Change – that was the answer to the problem. She would change *herself*! She would transform herself from a Spanish dancer and become an American film star instead.

CALL ME MARGARITA JEKYL!

Margarita threw herself into new acting lessons and speech classes. She worked day and night. There were times when she thought her efforts were a waste of time but at last, they began to pay off. Margarita spoke to herself at every opportunity, getting used to her new voice and her new accent. Her acting was improving, she was sounding American, but what good was that when she still looked Spanish?

Margarita took a long look at herself in the mirror. Everything was fine, except for her hair. It was black and curly and grew from a low hairline that really emphasized her Spanish looks. She had to do something about her hairline. If she couldn't change it, her plan was doomed.

Margarita had come so far that she wasn't going to turn back now. Drastic action was called for. That very day, she booked an appointment at a beauty salon and submitted herself to torture by electrolysis. Each hair from her hairline was individually removed and every follicle on her forehead was destroyed.

The slow, painful process continued for over two years until, at last, it was finished. There was just one final touch to be applied – auburn hair dye. When Margarita stared at herself in the mirror, she could hardly believe her eyes. The transformation was complete. She had managed to change herself totally. Gone was the accent, gone were her Spanish looks, there was only more thing to lose – her name.

No longer typecast as a Spanish dancer, the actress was almost immediately offered film roles. A few years later, in 1941, she got her first starring role opposite the brilliant James Cagney (1899–1986) and in the same year she was rehired by 20th Century Fox on five times her normal salary. Soon she was starring with Fred Astaire and Gene Kelly and she went on to enjoy many years as a Hollywood star. The end of Margarita Carmen Dolores Cansino marked the start of a great film career for – Rita Hayworth.

Cutting edge

Margarita Cansino's makeover got her career off to a flying start but lots of stars find it tough staying at the top. Nowadays, modern stars often have medical makeovers. They tend to keep quiet about what they've had done but Cher makes no bones about how she has managed to keep her career at the cutting edge.

Costing a mere snip at £24,000, Cher has had over thirteen operations. Her nose proved not to be up to the job until she had it slimmed down and shortened. Beauty wasn't skin deep until her acne scars were removed. Cher braced herself for close-ups by having braces put on her teeth. The movie star took it on the chin with a silicon implant and her sculpted cheekbones really were sculpted – by a plastic surgeon.

Method madness

There aren't many people who are willing to go as far as Cher or Rita Hayworth to be stars, but once actors have been cast in a film, they have used some fairly mad methods to get into their part.

1 To prepare for his part in *Last of the Mohicans*, Daniel Day-Lewis enrolled on a weapons training course and ran for miles with a musket strapped to his back. He also went on a woodlands survival course where he learnt to trap and skin animals.

2 One actor was so involved in playing his part as a doctor that when there was an accident in the street outside, he rushed out to help the accident victim. It was only when he had reached the injured person's side that he remembered that he didn't have a clue what to do.

3 Very few stars are willing to inflict as much pain on themselves as Neil Diamond did when he was shooting the remake of *The Jazz Singer*. In order to work himself up into a boiling rage, he asked his band to play him something that would make him furious. After a perfect take, the director asked him what the band had played and he replied, "A Barry Manilow number."

4 Not all groovy stars agree with these sorts of actor's antics. During the 1976 film, *Marathon Man*, Dustin Hoffman ran around the block so that he would appear breathless in the next scene. His co-star was British actor, Laurence Olivier, who was one of the most famous actors ever. Olivier was not very impressed by this activity and when Hoffman appeared at the end of his run, he simply suggested:

Film fashion

Movie stars look great so it's hardly surprising that film fans want to copy them. Of course, this isn't always a good idea and you may find some fashion fiascos lurking about in the back of your family's wardrobe. Why not ask your dad about that flared white suit that looks just like the one John Travolta wore in *Saturday Night Fever* and what about your sister's Pocahontas outfit? Get some photos now and they might come in useful in a few years time.

Amaze your sartorially-challenged teachers with your film fashion knowledge as you challenge them to take

1 Films shot in California started a new fashion in the 1920s. What did trendy men-about-town have to wear to get the new "California look"? Was it...?

a director's outfits
b soft shirt collars
c baseball hats

IT'S THE CALIFORNIA LOOK!

2 When Marlene Dietrich starred in *Morocco* in 1930, her appearance caused a storm of outrage because of something she was wearing. What item of clothing caused this fashion furore?

a a pair of trousers
b a pair of silk stockings
c a beret

OR AN INFLATABLE MACHINE GUN!

3 During the Second World War, the RAF named an item of equipment after the film star, Mae West. This piece of equipment is known to have saved hundreds of airmen's lives, but what is a "Mae West"?

a a parachute
b a machine gun
c an inflatable life jacket

4 After Clark Gable starred in *It Happened One Night* in 1934, sales of a certain type of men's clothing plummetted by forty per cent. What had suddenly became so unpopular?

a hats
b vests
c braces

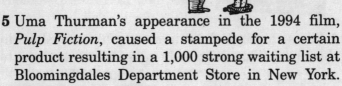

5 Uma Thurman's appearance in the 1994 film, *Pulp Fiction*, caused a stampede for a certain product resulting in a 1,000 strong waiting list at Bloomingdales Department Store in New York. What were film fans trying to buy?

a black bobbed wigs
b pairs of earrings
c a new nail varnish

Some movie stars have singlehandedly (or single-footedly) started whole new fashions. Can you match the star to the trend they began?

6 Elvis Presley   **a** Bobbed hair
7 Louise Brooks   **b** Leather motorbike jacket
8 Marlon Brando   **c** Tight trousers

Multiple choice answers

1-b Hollywood actors abandoned stiff collared shirts because they were uncomfortable in the Californian heat.

2-a In the 1930s, it was as unusual for women to wear trousers as it was for men to wear skirts. After Deitrich's appearance in trousers, women's fashion changed, although it's still hard to find men wearing skirts – unless they're Scottish!

3-c There is only one other movie person who has given their name to something. Busby Berkeley was a famous dance choreographer and a "Busby Berkeley" is a very elaborate musical number.

4-b Clark Gable's bare chest knocked the spots off vests.

5-c The nail varnish was called Rouge Noir. It was a brand new shade of black and customers couldn't wait to get their hands (and nails) on it.

6-c Rock 'n' roll and movie star Elvis Presley wore tight trousers at the start his career, launching thousands of imitators. By the end of his career however, no one was copying his clothes – and it's not hard to see why.

HE MAY BE THE KING OF ROCK 'N' ROLL, BUT AT FASHION HE'S A JESTER

7-a Silent movie star Louise Brooks was happy with her brand-new hair style but she was a bit more shy about wearing trousers – she only wore them indoors.

8-b Bikers went wild after Marlon Brando appeared as a leather-jacketed biker in *The Wild One* in 1954.

Shooting stars

A lot of people think that acting is a doddle, until they try it that is. If you've ever had to pretend that you're enjoying your dad's Elvis impression or your English teacher's star Shakespearean turn, it makes you realize the secret of a good actor. They make a difficult job look easy.

Movie stars don't just turn up to say a few words then get back to lounging around a swimming pool. Shooting a movie sounds groovy but it isn't just difficult, sometimes it can be downright grotty. Some stars deserve danger money for some of things they have had to put with:

1 The monstrous make-up that turned John Hurt into the Elephant Man in 1980 took a marathon *seven hour* session to apply. When it was complete, the actor wasn't able to eat for the rest of the day.

2 In 1991 the cast of *Alive* had to suffer an even

more dastardly diet. This movie tells the real-life, revolting tale of how the starving survivors of a crashed plane managed to stay alive – by developing a taste for cannibalism. During filming, the actors were put on a crash diet so they could really look as if they were starving. To add to the tastebud torture, they also had to watch the film crew eating huge meals right in front of them.

3 Dustin Hoffman fought off an attack of the killer costumes when he was acting in the 1992 film, *Hook*. His pirate costume was so hot and heavy that the star had to wear an air-conditioned jacket, originally designed to be worn by astronauts in deep space, underneath it.

4 Some of the cast of *Star Wars* could have done with some similar space-age technology. The actor playing Chewbacca got heatstroke in his clammy costume, while the Imperial Storm Troopers had problems walking, let alone storming anywhere. Their helmets were so badly designed that they could hardly see out of them and they kept bumping into each other. The killer costume won by a knockout in one incident when an actor was knocked cold after colliding with another storm trooper.

LUCKY YOU WERE WEARING THOSE HELMETS OR YOU MIGHT HAVE GOT HURT!

5 Peter O'Toole's heroic performance as Lawrence of Arabia in 1962 was especially heroic considering what happened to him when he was making the film. He didn't have a stunt double and during shooting, he almost fractured his skull, strained most of his muscles, was bitten by a camel and suffered third-degree sunburn.

6 News that the 1967 musical *Dr Dolittle* was going to be filmed at Castle Combe had an explosive effect on one of the village residents. Sir Ranulph Twistleton-Wykeham Fiennes (who later became

a famous explorer) decided to protect his home territory from the invading movie makers by planting bombs in various strategic spots around the village. Two bombs actually exploded before Sir Ranulph was arrested. The film's cast and crew spent the first day of production treading very carefully while the bomb squad searched for more devices. Eventually, Sir Ranulph was "Fienned" £500.

MOVIES ARE ONLY SUPPOSED TO 'BOMB' AT THE BOX OFFICE! GUILTY!

7 Shooting the 1954 movie *20,000 Leagues Under the Sea* proved to be downright dangerous for the film's star, James Mason. During a fight scene with a giant squid the star was dragged underwater. At first, the movie crew were impressed by his convincing portrayal of a drowning man until someone realized that he wasn't acting – he was actually drowning. Luckily, the star was dragged onto solid ground and he was revived in the nick of time.

BRILLIANT! YOU DESERVE AN OSCAR!

I'D RATHER HAVE A LIFEBELT!

Awful actors

Acting can have an awful effect on some people. If one of your friends has been in the school play, you may have noticed some of the changes. Big, swollen head, loud behaviour and hugging other actors are all classic symptoms of a disorder called *hammingitupitis actoris*.

These symptoms normally wear off a few months after the moment of fame has passed, but imagine what a lifetime of stardom can do to actors. From *hammingitupitis actoris*, they progress to *tempertantrums horribilis* and then onto *egomania superstaritis*. Having reached this stage, there is no going back to normal behaviour. You might think that some of the things your little brother does are a pain, but stars suffering from *egomania superstaritis* are much, much worse.

1 British star Rex Harrison acted the perfect gentleman on-screen in *Dr Doolittle* but off it behaved so badly that the crew nicknamed him Tyrannosaurus Rex.

GRR!

I CAN TALK TO THE ANIMALS BUT NOT TO THAT MONSTER!

2 After starring with Kirk Douglas in a movie, Burt Lancaster said, "Kirk would be the first person to tell you he's a difficult man. I would be the second." Director Richard Fleischer would be the third. When shooting the 1958 movie *The Vikings* with Kirk Douglas, the star held up shooting by

complaining that he couldn't get comfortable. The director eventually worked out what the problem was. The awful actor only felt "comfortable" if he was right in the centre of every single shot.

3 The jokes in the 1959 classic comedy, *Some Like it Hot*, come at the audience thick and fast – unlike the shooting of the film. Marilyn Monroe had so much trouble saying her lines that her co-stars used to bet on how many takes she would need to get through her dialogue. She did 59 takes of one scene in which she only had to say three words: "Where's the Bourbon?"

4 Orson Welles and Peter Sellers disliked each other so much that they refused to act together in a scene in the 1967 movie, *Casino Royale*. Each star was eventually filmed on alternate days acting with a stand-in.

5 Julia Roberts behaved so awfully during the making of *Pretty Woman* that her co-star, Richard Gere, started a club called the "I survived working with Julia Roberts club". Gere wrote out a list of his awful experiences with the actress and handed it on to Roberts' next leading man. The list was then added to and handed on … and on … and on.

Silly stories and celluloid scandals

Most people are delighted to get their name in the papers (even if it is spelt wrong) but movie makers and film actors aren't always happy at getting star billing – especially if it's their monstrous movies or awful acting that's hitting the headlines.

Newshounds are constantly trying to sniff out the latest movie stories and they will go to some surprising lengths to get them. All but *one* of the following silly stories and celluloid scandals appeared in print. Read them carefully then use your investigative powers to decide which one never made it to the front page.

Shameful Snog

By our cinematographic correspondent

The offending Kiss that shocked the audience.

Never did I think that films would stoop this low. As a reviewer of moving pictures for the past two years, I was horrified to see something so absolutely disgusting. I am referring of course, to the scene in *The Widow Jones* in which the audience is subjected to a close-up kiss between the two leading actors. I feel most strongly that this is inappropriate behaviour to be shown to the public in this year of 1896.

Toilet Terror

Actors sighed "what a relief" while critics shouted "what an outrage" at the release of *The Crowd* in 1928. The film's director appeared flushed with success after the premiere, claiming that the audience had been bowled over by his movie in which a toilet appears on screen for the first time.

Loo role. Lavatory panned by the critics.

THE DAILY BLAH

STAR SENTENCE

Ear today, gaol tomorrow? Clark Gable avoiding photographers at court today.

In a sensational appearance today, Clark Gable, the King of Hollywood, arrived in court to plead guilty to killing a pedestrian while drunk driving. An informant has told this court that Mr Gable had been drinking heavily at a Hollywood party before leaving in his car. While on his way home, he rounded a corner too fast, lost control and knocked the unfortunate woman over.

Sentencing of the star is expected to take place tomorrow.

BIN MEN GET BINNED

Has-bins. The garbage men canned today.

Joan Collins' refuse collectors found a surprising sack waiting for them when they went round to the movie star's Los Angeles mansion – they were fired. Ms Collins defended her decision, saying that she had given the men the sack when she discovered that they had been sorting through her rubbish in the hope of selling off souvenirs or scandalous material.

Of course, all they found was a load of old garbage.

'I never took anything' says sacked bin man.

Answer

The only story that never appeared is the one concerning Clark Gable. The article tells the true story of a drink driving accident that actually happened but the scandal was hushed up and was never reported.

Clark Gable did not appear in court because he was protected by Louis B. Meyer, the boss of the MGM film studio. Meyer could not afford for his biggest star to go to prison so he told Gable to lie low while he sorted things out. Meyer carefully chose a studio employee and offered him an unusual deal. The employee would be given a job and an income for life if he did Mr Meyer just one small favour. The man agreed to lie to the court and swear that he had been driving the car while Gable was in the passenger seat. The MGM employee got just one year in prison for reckless driving while the star got away with murder.

The final curtain

When it comes to keeping up appearances, movie stars beat everyone – even big sisters. Their image is extremely important and they don't just hog the bathroom, they hog entire beauty salons and keep whole publicity departments busy. Stars keep up their image all their lives and even when the final curtain goes down on them, some of them are determined to go out in true Hollywood style.

Rudolph Valentino wasn't a great actor but he was a great screen idol of the 1920s. He specialized in playing wildly romantic heroes and had several huge successes. The mysterious depth of his on-screen gazes was actually due to the fact that he was short-sighted but the studio wouldn't allow him to wear glasses in case it ruined his image. The studio publicists also decided that his real name, Rodolpho Guglielmio, was not nearly romantic enough so they made one up. The new, improved version of the star's name was Rodolpho Alfonzo Rafaelo Pierre Filibert Guglielmio di Valentina d'Antonguolla – or Rudy for short!

Unfortunately for Rudy, his career didn't last anywhere as long his new name. He died in 1926 at the age of 31, at the height of his success. Several fans committed suicide at the news of his death which meant that they missed an even more spectacular event. Normally, funerals are sad, solemn affairs, but Valentino was one star who wasn't going quietly. Among the highlights were:

- Thousands of spectators lining the route to the cemetery.
- A low flying plane dropping flowers from the sky.
- Wreath sent by Italian dictator, Benito Mussolini.
- Charlie Chaplin acting as one of the pall-bearers.
- Silent film star Pola Negri bursting through the mourners, claiming that she had been secretly engaged to Valentino.
- A commemorative song called "There's a new star in heaven tonight" being played during the star-studded show, er, funeral.

IT'S SO SAD – HIS FUNERAL'S A SMASH HIT, BUT HE CAN'T DO A SEQUEL!

Valentino's appeal continued long after he had been buried. Every year until 1954, a mysterious woman in black placed a white rose on Valentino's grave on the anniversary of his death.

Funeral facts

When you've acted all your life, why let a little thing like death get in the way of your performance? Some stars just don't know when to stop. Test yourself in this mini:

MOVIE BUFF-BUSTER

QUIZ No. 4

1 Bella Lugosi became a big star after appearing as Count Dracula in 1931. When he died, he was

buried with:
a his Dracula cape
b his Dracula fangs
c a bottle of blood

2 Legendary swash-buckling movie star, Errol Flynn, was buried with:
a A pirate cutlass
b Two boxes of cigars
c Six crates of whisky

Multiple Choice Answers

1-a Maybe Bella Lugosi (who was actually born in Transylvania) thought he would rise from the grave. He didn't of course, but his career has been resurrected with repeated showings of his films.

2-c Errol Flynn was only fifty when he died. Surprisingly for a star who had lead such a colourful and notorious life, one of his early jobs had been as a policeman.

ANIMAL ANTICS

So what are your options if you want to get into the groovy movie world but you don't want a starring role yourself? Why not try checking out the family for some star talent. Your brother would be good in a monster movie, but on second thoughts, that might be going too far – you don't want to scare the audience too much. Maybe there is one other animal in the family you should audition. How about Fido, the trusty family dog.

It's not as barking mad an idea as you might think. Some Hollywood pets *do* win prizes and the following diary makes no bones about it – but don't let Fido get his paws on it or he'll never be happy with his old basket again.

Diary of a 1920s film star

07:00
Woken up at the crack of dawn. I was feeling crumpled after a bad night's sleep so my personal valet spent some time brushing my hair before I was ready to face everyone.

GOING ANYWHERE NICE FOR YOUR HOLIDAYS THIS YEAR?

JUST HOW I LIKE IT, RAW

07:30
Wolfed down a light breakfast prepared by my personal chef. Chef's main concern is to provide me with a nutritious

start to the day. It helps me keep fit and in shape - mustn't disappoint the fans, you know.

07:45 *Checked myself in the mirror. Looking good and feeling trim despite overindulging with my favourite chocolate buttons last night.*

08:00 *Car arrived to drive me to the studio. It's going to be a perfect day for filming, I can smell it in the air. The new chauffeur turned out to be a complete idiot and took the long way round. I'm afraid that I rather barked at him when he took the wrong turning.*

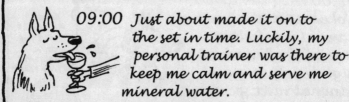

09:00 *Just about made it on to the set in time. Luckily, my personal trainer was there to keep me calm and serve me mineral water.*

11:00 *Film sets are so dull. I've just been hanging around while the director sets up some shots. I went on set and spotted some familiar faces in the crowd. I'm so glad I'm not an extra, the way they're treated* is inhuman. As I wasn't needed, I padded back to my five dressing rooms.

11:30 Went through my scene with the director until he was satisfied. He's a real slave driver. He seems to think that when he whistles, everyone should jump to it. Luckily, it's not too difficult. I haven't got any lines today, I've just got to react to a fellow actor then make my moves. Trainer was there to keep an eye on everything.

13:15 It's a wrap! Shooting's over for the day. Everyone said I was marvellous and made such a fuss of me. I don't have trouble on set, acting comes naturally to me - it's just like an animal instinct.

14:00 Chef's done himself proud again. I invited my trainer to join me and we both settled down together for a splendid lunch. He seems very pleased with how my career is going and told me some great news - I have had another pay rise. I'm now on $1,000 a week. That should keep the wolf from the door for a while.

14:30 Trainer's been discussing some new ideas with me. It seems that my old screen rival Strongheart has just published his own book called Letters to Strongheart and he thinks we should do the same. I'm not convinced myself, I think he's barking up the wrong tree.

15:30 I've just enjoyed a quiet few minutes alone in my dressing room and found my mind wandering back to the early days. Movies were silent when I began and I can still remember going for the talkie test. I was so nervous until I heard that technician muttering that you can't teach an old dog new tricks. I'll show them, I thought, and indeed I did. Though I say it myself, I think I've made the transition to sound with only a few hairy moments.

15:35 I was roused from my thoughts with the surprise news that I have been booked to make a personal appearance. I was hoping for a short rest but I mustn't let my fans down. I will continue with my diary on my return.

18:00 Home at last! Am feeling dog tired but what a wonderful afternoon. I could smell that something was up when we pulled up outside the movie theatre. I didn't know I had so many fans. My valet had worked wonders in the limousine and I was looking sleek and well-groomed.

19:30 Chef produced another fine dinner - filet mignon steak cut into small cubes - delicious. One of my sons joined us for the meal and announced that he too was hoping to make it in the movie business - what a young pup he is.

MANNERS!

20:30 Been for a good long walk with my trainer. I'm not allowed out on my own any more in case I get kidnapped. Such are the perils of fame. Still, soon I was back to air-conditioned comfort, chef's special evening snack and a good brushing from the valet. These humans have this saying about it being a dog's life but it seems pretty groovy to me.

Rin Tin Tin

Animal stars

Not many animal stars are treated as well as famous dog film star Rin Tin Tin, but not many stars have saved an entire studio. The greatest rescue he ever made was in the 1920s when his films saved 20th Century Fox from bankruptcy.

When Rinty took his final bow wow-wow in 1932, his puppies were in demand. Luckily for Rin Tin Tin Junior, he was wanted for his acting abilities, not for his skill as a watchdog. In 1936, he starred in a film called *The Canine Detective*. During the movie, he captured an entire gang of robbers. A few months after the film came out, a gang of burglars broke into the home of his owner and stole many valuable items. Rin Tin Tin Junior slept throughout the entire raid, proving just how good an actor he really was!

Dumb actors quiz

Whole herds of animal stars have invaded Hollywood. Animals may not be able to talk but they can do lots of things that human stars can't. Why not test your friends to see if they know their Hollywood pets from Hollywood pests? Are they are tough enough to take on the:

Match the famous film stars to their on-screen antics.

1 Clyde the orang-utan teamed up with Clint Eastwood in *Every Which Way But Loose* in 1978. What was Clyde's killer speciality?

2 Trigger was known as the world's smartest horse. He starred in over a hundred films including *Gone with the Wind* and *The Lone Ranger* but he didn't do much horsing around. According to one human actor, what star quality did he possess?

3 Flipper the Dolphin was described as a "ham from the word go". The success of *Flipper* in 1963 led to a long-running (or should that be long-swimming) TV series. What underwater antic did this aquatic "ham" perfect?

4 Cheetah the chimpanzee played opposite Tarzan in 1918. When he wasn't monkeying around, what were his on screen specialities?

5 Hooch the slobbery dog starred with Tom Hanks
in the 1990s' shaggy dog tale, *Turner and Hooch*.
Which of his animal antics gave his co-star paws
for thought during shooting?

a sub-aqua somersaults
b he could give cuddles and carry messages
c he played dead when someone shouted "bang"
d he could soak a clean shirt in 10 minutes
e he required less takes than human actors

1-c, 2-e, 3-a, 4-b, 5-d

Answers:

Terrible Tales

For some movie makers, acting with animals can
turn out to be a real howler. Working with animal
stars – even Trigger – doesn't guarantee an easy
ride and they can get up to all sorts of monkey
business on set. *Did you know...?*

1 When it comes to awful acting, Braveheart, a top
dog of the 1920s, really took the biscuit. He hated
howling so much that he would sulk for days
afterwards if he had to do it. Eventually things got
so bad that a dog double was brought in to howl
for him.

2 Donald O'Connor was delighted at the success of
the six films he had made with Francis the talking
mule in the 1930s. He was less delighted when he
discovered that Francis was getting more mail

than him and he refused to do any more films with his four-legged co-star – a case of the mule making an ass of the actor.

3 An immovable problem faced the director of a western in 1941. The script of *Western Union* called for a herd of cattle to be stampeded, but the cows were refusing to budge. Gunshots had proved to be unreliable in the past, so the entire shoot ground to a halt. Eventually, one of the crew remembered seeing German Stukas divebombing in a newsreel and suggested that they try the same tactic. A squadron of aircraft was called up and the herd was duly divebombed. It worked! The cows took off and so did the film at the box office.

4 A hair-raising problem played havoc with the filming of the first Lassie film. The film was being shot during summer and a female dog was playing the faithful hound. Unfortunately, no one realized

that female collies shed their coats in summer! To avoid canine continuity catastrophes, only male collies have starred as Lassie since then.

5 Sometimes, owners can be as beastly as their animals. When Trigger appeared in the 1946 movie, *Ziegfield Follies*, his tail had been braided and his mane decorated with pink satin bows. The owner saw red at the pink bows and threatened the studio with court action.

When movie makers have reached the end of their tether with animal antics and when the thought of awful actors gives them stars in front of the eyes, there's only one place to go – back to the drawing board.

Awesome animators have produced some of the funkiest film stars on their drawing boards, and cartoon creations certainly have some advantages over real life stars. Their crazy capers are confined to the screen. There's no awful acting or beastly behaviour to put up with.

AN A-Z OF CARTOON CAPERS

A Animators who have done other jobs. When his studio was starting work on *Dumbo*, Walt Disney asked if any of his staff had any circus experience. To his amazement, he discovered that one of the directors had been a trick rider, a studio guide was a juggler, an animator had been on the high wire while a mild-mannered typist owned up to having been a lion tamer.

Betty Boop. She first came to life in 1930 but not as we know her now. Originally, she looked like a long-eared dog because she was meant to be the canine companion of a dog called Bimbo. After two years, these design blips were blooped out and the new look Betty boop-oop-a-dooped her way to success as the first speaking and singing cartoon character.

Changing the story. Disney's animated movie *Pocahontas* had little to do with the Indian princess in real life. Can you spot the differences between the animated version and the actual version?

1 The Powhatan Princess was awesomely brave when she saved the life of the British settler, John Smith, but she was a very young girl at the time.

2 Pocahontas wore the latest in Powhatan scarecuts – her head was shaved.

3 She didn't fall in love with John Smith.

4 Three years after John Smith returned to England, she fell in love with and married a different settler called John Rolfe.

D Walt Disney, the King of Cartoons. His awesome animation achievements include:

- Producing the first sound cartoon called *Steamboat Willie*, starring Mickey Mouse.
- Making *Snow White*, the world's first animated feature film in colour.
- Winning an awesomely large number of Oscars.

Among the awesome advances his studio made was the multiplane camera. If the instructions on a disposable camera leave you baffled, this monster would have your mind boggling. Standing nearly five metres tall and costing $70,000 to build in 1937, this larger than life invention enabled the camera to look through various "planes" – giving depth and dimension to shots. It was so complicated to use that two engineering graduates were constantly kept busy working out the mathematics involved in drawing and photographing each sequence.

As well as running his studio, Walt also found time to build the first Disneyland theme park where his animated characters could come to life.

E "Eeh, what's up, doc?". Bugs Bunny's famous catchphrase was changed from the scripted "What's cookin'?"

F Felix the cat. This black cat appeared in 1919 and was certainly lucky for his creator, Pat Sullivan. Felix was designed to be quick to draw (being solid black saved drawing outlines) and his creator was quick on the draw to make money out of his cartoon capers.

G Ghost. Casper the Friendly Ghost first materialized in 1945. He haunted his way through a regular TV series and his career really lifted off when he appeared in 3-D on the moon in *Boo Moon* before spooking big screen viewers in 1995.

H Ray Harryhausen. Harryhausen was a monstrously talented animator who specialized in mixing his animated monsters with live action. This process is awesomely awkward and can bring tears to the eyes – as one actor discovered in the 1973 movie, *The Golden Voyage of Sinbad.*

The actor was scripted to fight a duel with one of Harryhausen's horrors – a six-armed Indian goddess. Before filming, Harryhausen strapped together three stuntmen to rehearse the fight with the actor. The actor had to memorize his moves with the stunt-beetle and then he would be filmed shadow fighting. Unfortunately, the fight sequence was so complicated that the actor couldn't remember his moves. He got so muddled that he just sat down and started to cry, proving that acting with animated monsters isn't 'armless fun at all.

I Insurance. In 1939, the Fleischer Studio took out a $185,000 policy to insure the hands of all the 116 animators who were working on their feature film, *Mr Bug Goes to Town*.

J *Jurassic Park*. This monster success of a movie was due to a clever mix of dinosaur models and computer animation. Animators had an awesome choice of almost 17 million shades to help them match the colours of their animated creations with the models.

HONESTLY DARLING — THAT SHADE OF GREEN IS SO UNFASHIONABLE!

COLOUR CHART

K Koko the Clown. He was the first character to combine live action with animation. In 1919, Koko appeared out of his cartoonist's inkpot or pen nib before clowning around in the live settings around the drawing board.

L Disney's *The Lion King*. Simba the lion is king of the jungle and king at the box office too. To guarantee that the movie was a roaring success, lions were brought into the studio so the animators could copy their movements.

M Mickey Mouse. In 1933, he received 800,000 fan letters, making him the most popular movie star ever. He was once described as "America's one and only contribution to world culture".

N Ninja Turtles. What have these half-shelled heroes got in common with Dick Tracy, Batman and Superman? Is it…?

1 they all eat pizzas.
2 their real names are all connected with famous artists.
3 they are all characters who have moved from cartoons to the big screen.

O *One Hundred and One Dalmatians*. The animated version of the book by Dodie Smith was released in 1961 but it seems that audiences are quite happy to see spots in front of their eyes. A new, live action version starring Glenn Close as the awesomely awful Cruella de Vil was filmed in 1996. It's just as well it isn't a sequel – can you imagine 202 Dalmatians?

P *Pantomimis Lumineuses*. These forerunners of the animated cartoon were invented in 1892 by Emile Reynaud. He painted his animations on film strips then projected them on a special machine. The movie pioneer later starred in his own private pantomime when he allegedly went a little mad and threw his machine into the Seine.

Q Quacking. Donald Duck's scripts were translated into seven languages and each word spelt out phonetically. Then, Clarence Nash, the voice of Donald Duck, would quack his lines in each language – a clear case of an animaniac going animal quackers.

R Rouge. Animators had an awesome task trying to find the correct colour for Snow White's face in the classic 1937 cartoon. Eventually, the problem was solved when they dabbed rouge on her cheeks.

S Seven Dwarfs. Awesome animator, Walt Disney made lots of good decisions and one of the best was to change his mind – seven times. If he hadn't done so, Snow White's co-stars would have been called Blabby, Hotsy, Biggy-Wiggy, Weepy, Jaunty, Biggo-Ego and Awful.

Tunnel. In 1939, there was terrific rivalry between two animation studios, the Walt Disney Studios in Hollywood and the Fleischer Studio in Miami. So many animators were lured away to Disney that a story started doing the rounds that the Fleischer Studio had been built over an old railway tunnel that came up in the Disney Studios.

U"Unfortunately, animation is a slow business." It can take Nick Park and his animators as long as a week to film ten seconds of Wallace and Gromit's adventures. Mouths are especially difficult and Wallace had several sets of teeth showing different widths of grins and about a dozen mouth shapes. Luckily, Wallace brought a smile to Nick Park's lips when his creations won two Oscars.

VVirtual Reality. The 1996 film, *Toy Story*, is the first film to be entirely computer animated. The toys only existed in virtual reality and although it looks as though they appeared on set together, they never actually did. The same was true of the stars who voiced the two main parts. Although it sounds like they were acting together, they never actually did. Tom Hanks (Woody the cowboy) recorded his scenes in Los Angeles while Tim Allen voiced Buzz Lightyear in Detroit.

W Robin Williams. This comic genius voiced the part of the genie in the 1993 film, *Aladdin*. The movie makers let the mad-cap motormouth throw away the script and ad-lib his way through the story. They then animated the Genie's antics around the new script.

X Xeroxing process. This was another of Disney's awesomely useful inventions. The process copied cartoon characters and helped speed up animation. Without it, the studio would never have considered the appallingly awful task of making a film with one hundred and one characters!

Y "You can be an animator too." Take a book and draw a simple picture in the top right hand corner of a page. Turn the page and draw the same picture with a small change. Continue to do this until you have finished then flick through the book to watch your very own cartoon capers. These flick books have always been popular, and in 1896, one inventive animator added a flipping lever to the book and patented his invention as The Filoscope.

Z Robert Zemeckis, the director of *Who Framed Roger Rabbit*? Zemeckis dreamt up a complicated mixture of live action and comic capers, not realizing it would have a serious effect on the film's star, Bob Hoskins. For almost all of the six month shoot, Hoskins had to act with a cast of imaginary cartoon characters. Not surprisingly, he ended up seeing things. He only recovered when his doctor ordered him to take a long break.

Name:

Age: It's hard to be precise. Hollywood's as old as the rest of California.

I don't think you understand. When did movie makers move to Hollywood? Oh, I see. The first Hollywood studio was built in 1911 but film pioneers had arrived in California a few years earlier.

What did it look like? In those days, it was a teetotal colony consisting of a few houses and orange groves.

And now? It's a rather grotty part of Los Angeles.

Why did the movie makers choose Hollywood? The answer's summed up by the film phrase, *lights, camera, action*.

I don't quite follow. What have lights got to do with it? Early movie makers needed natural light. In New York, they had to film on top of buildings to catch as much daylight as possible.

And that caused problems? You bet. Filming was often stopped when it rained or snowed. In high winds, the sets used to wobble and then there was the bird problem.

They used to fly onto the set? And worse. Use your imagination.

Oh yuk! Exactly. California offered good weather all year round and a wide range of locations that were perfect for movie makers.

Got it. So what was the deal with cameras? Thomas Edison and the biggest movie companies patented the mechanism of film cameras. Anyone else who wanted to make a film had to pay them large amounts of money.

And these people didn't want to hand over the money? Exactly. Independent movie makers continued filming but didn't cough up.

What happened next? Edison's Patents Company were unhappy about not getting paid, so the Patents War began.

It wasn't a real war, was it? Well, the Patents Company used some fairly brutal methods to stop the independents.

Such as? They hired gangsters to burn down their studios and to destroy their cameras. Their favourite method was shooting holes at the camera. Even if the bullets missed the machine, they would probably hit the cameraman or the director.

So how did moving to Hollywood help? It was very remote and the independents hoped that it would be out of range of the Patent Enforcers.

And was it? On the whole, yes, although director Cecil B. DeMille was shot at.

Did that stop him? No, he carried on filming and bought a wolf to guard the negatives.

He sounds barking mad. He may have been but the wolf worked – he wasn't bothered again.

That just leaves "action". What sort of action are we talking about here? Trade union action.

You mean strikes and things? Correct. Movie makers wanted to avoid trade unions. There were none in Hollywood and the result was that labour costs were half those in New York.

So movie making was cheaper in Hollywood? You've got it. There was a plentiful supply of extras and sometimes local people would act for free – just for the fun of it. Studios would then hold a free film viewing for everyone who had appeared in it.

Those were the days, eh? They certainly were.

Studio stories

In the first days of film, it was quite simple to set up your very own studio – because studios were dead simple. Instead of the gleaming groovy buildings that you see nowadays, early movie makers rented out barns or shops. They emptied the building, gathered some friends and equipment together, painted the name of their film company on the door and that was it – the studio was ready!

It was so easy that studios sprang up all over the world and a "reel" revolution began. Studios were like film factories – the more films they churned out, the bigger they got. The bigger they got the more money they made and the more staff they took on. The more staff they employed, the bigger their wage bill. The bigger the wage bill, they more films they had to make. The more films they made, the bigger they got...

Studio questions

The studios that succeeded soon gobbled up the competition, making themselves even larger. Challenge your friends and see if they're big enough to take on the studios in:

MOVIE BUFF-BUSTER

QUIZ NO. 6

1 The first film studio was built in 1893 by Thomas Edison. What was it nicknamed?
a The Tardis
b The Movie Booth
c The Black Maria

I'M MAKING LAST YEAR'S BIG SMASH

STUDIO

2 Which of the following facilities did Hollywood studios *not* provide:
a train stations
b hospitals
c private police forces

CRASH!

CUT!

3 MGM's slogan was:
a The biggest, brightest and the best
b More stars than there are in the heavens
c The future of film

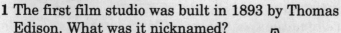

AUTOGRAPHS

4 Paramount used to test their films by:
a showing them in prisons
b previewing them in schools
c showing them to the boss's children

WELL?

5 British studio, Rank, was originally formed to make:
a religious films

b propaganda films
c wildlife films

6 Which famous groovy movie maker founded The Dreamworks studio? Is it...?
a Robin Williams
b George Lucas
c Steven Spielberg

Multiple choice answers

1-c The Black Maria was a small, tar-paper hut. It had a roof that opened to let in the sun and was pivoted so it could be turned around to catch the light.

2-a By the 1920s, studios were like small cities. As well as hospitals and their own police forces, they also had schools, barber shops and fire departments, although they didn't have train stations.

3-b MGM's stars included Clark Gable, Elizabeth Taylor, Greta Garbo and Lassie.

4-c Some studios weren't that bothered about audience or critics' reactions. Jack Warner once said, "Today's newspaper is tomorrow's toilet paper".

5-a Rank's prayers were answered when it became the biggest British studio, flourishing before the Second World War.

6-c Steven Spielberg is not the only movie maker to found a studio. In 1919, Charlie Chaplin joined forces with Mary Pickford, Douglas Fairbanks and D.W. Griffith to set up United Artists.

Movie moguls

The men in charge of the movie studios were called moguls. They were the most powerful men in Hollywood, ruling over their studios like emperors. They were tougher than old boots and would make even your headteacher look as soft as a melting blancmange. This ghastly group had some strange habits and anyone meeting them needed some wise words of warning.

Don't be surprised – Max Sennet, who produced the *Keystone Cops* movies had a bath tub installed in his office. Walt Disney used to borrow wild animals from zoos and bring them into his studios for animators to observe. Darryl Zanuck, head of 20th Century Fox, used to swing a polo mallet during meetings and he once asked for a one page synopsis of *War and Peace*, one of the longest novels ever written.

Don't interrupt and **don't** argue – Darryl Zanuck hated his monologues being interrupted. His order to one employee was, "Don't say yes until I've finished."

Don't get on the wrong side of a movie mogul – Harry Cohn, the founder of Columbia pictures, boasted, "I don't get ulcers, I give them." Louis B. Meyer, head honcho at MGM, was once compared to an elephant except that "... Meyer's diet is his fellow man."

... AND I DON'T WORK FOR PEANUTS

Don't say the wrong thing – Harry Cohn had film sets wired up so he could listen in on private conversations.

Don't be put off by what you hear – Samuel Goldwyn (who changed his surname from Goldfish) was famous for his Goldwynisms such as "Include me out ... a wide screen just makes a bad film twice as bad ... verbal contracts aren't worth the paper they're written on."

YOU CAN'T PROVE I SAID THAT UNLESS YOU'VE GOT IT IN WRITING!

Do watch where you sit – one of the chairs in Harry Cohn's dining room was wired to give an electric shock. And when a film producer sat down at the same table as the Warner Brothers without being invited, he was sacked on the spot.

Do be tough – if someone came to Louis B. Meyer with a complaint, the movie mogul used to cry until they backed down.

Do be clever when asking for a pay rise – movie moguls were famously mean with money but one actress worked out the perfect time to ask for a pay rise. In 1932, Joan Crawford demanded more money from Louis B. Meyer when the film she was making was almost complete. She couldn't be replaced and the movie couldn't be finished without her. Eventually she got what she wanted.

Do be careful during Christmas – Harry Cohn once offered a favourite secretary a special Christmas present: he would fire anyone she pointed at.

Crazy Contracts

Movie moguls ruled their empires with a rod of iron – and pieces of paper. But these were no ordinary pieces of paper. More fearsome than a French test, more lethal than any Latin exam, were the crazy contracts.

If an actor was lucky enough to get spotted by a studio, he or she would be offered a contract. At first sight, movie contracts looked groovy:

MOVIE STAR CONTRACT – Good points

1 The Studio will provide steady work for seven years.
2 The Studio will provide regular pay rises.
3 The star will be granted free access to all studio facilities including dance classes, diction classes and leisure facilities.

But a second look revealed a grotty version:

MOVIE STAR CONTRACT – Bad points

1 The Studio reserves the right to review this contract every six months. If the studio decides the star has not reached the required standard, this contract will be cancelled. The star cannot cancel the contract under any circumstances but must remain contracted to the Studio for the full seven years.

---

2 The Studio shall decide all parts and movies for the star. The star will have no choice in the matter.

3 Should the star refuse to act in any movie, this contract will be extended to cover the period of time that the film took to shoot.

4 Stars can be loaned to work for other studios but they will only be paid at their current contract rate.*

Crazy clauses

If that wasn't grotty enough, some stars had their own personalized crazy clauses:

1 In 1930, Joan Crawford's contract specified the exact time she had to go to bed!

I WON'T SIGN UNTIL YOU GUARANTEE HOT CHOCOLATE AS WELL!

2 Alice White's 1929 contract was even more ghastly. It told her that she couldn't get married and, most gruesome of all, that she had to go back to school to learn *two* foreign languages.

---

*This clause was one of the studios' greatest money spinners. Ingrid Bergman was loaned out by David Selznick eight times. When she appeared in *Gaslight* in 1944, she was paid her contract rate of $75,000 but the studio received $253,750 and pocketed the difference.

3 Signing a contract with MGM might have brought a smile to the lips of comedian Buster Keaton but he wasn't allowed to show it – not on screen anyway. His crazy clause specified that he must not be filmed smiling.

HAPPY WITH THE CONTRACT?

OVERJOYED

4 The entire cast of Cecil B. De Mille's 1927 film *King of Kings*, were not allowed to accept any roles without the director's approval for an entire decade but they got off lightly compared to the star of the film who wasn't even allowed to divorce her husband.

5 One star who was also a boxing fan was not allowed by Warner Brothers to shout during fights in case she strained her voice. Douglas Fairbanks Jnr's contract kept him grounded – he wasn't allowed to fly in a plane.

6 The studio which employed Johnny Weismuller, who played Tarzan, came up with a novel way of helping him to diet – a weight clause. At the beginning of each movie, the star had to weigh in at 190 lbs. For every pound overweight, he would be fined $5,000 up to a

YOU'RE A BIG STAR, BUT DON'T GET ANY BIGGER!

maximum of $50,000 dollars. The prospect of his salary being reduced by two thirds must have made Weismuller as sick as a parrot because he weighed in at precisely 189 lbs for each film.

Star slaves

With these sorts of crazy clauses, it's hardly surprising that some movie stars felt more like star slaves. In 1936, actress Bette Davis decided to fight the contract system and it turned into a battle royal with no holds barred.

Move 1: The overseas scuttle

After being offered a long string of bad parts by Warner Brothers, the actress defiantly travelled to London to act in two films.

Move 2: The court clutch

Jack Warner fought back by sueing her for breach of contract and the case was tried in London.

Move 3: Slave surprise

The star's barrister surprised the court by describing her fight as a battle against a lifetime of slavery.

Move 4: Witness protection

She then threw in a knockout blow by refusing to

---

call any witnesses. This prevented Jack Warner's barrister from cross-examining the actress to find out about her life as a star slave.

Move 5: Whirlwind wig

Jack Warner's barrister was so cross at this that he threw his wig across the court.

Move 6: Judgement day

At the end of the case, the judge decided that the contract was legally binding because the actress had signed it of her own free will.

Move 7: The sucker punch

The judge then awarded costs of $30,000 dollars against the beaten star.

Contract Killer

Although the studio won this battle, they didn't win the contract war. In 1944, Olivia de Havilland won her case against Warner Brothers and became the first contract killer. Within a few years, all the former star slaves had revolted. They decided to get their own back on the studios by drawing up some crazy clauses of their own.

1 Audrey Hepburn proved that she was no fashion victim in the 1983 movie, *Bloodline*. She not only insisted on having all her film costumes designed by the fashion designers, Givenchy, but her

contract also stated that she would be given all the clothes afterwards.

2 One movie star was such a cricket fan that the entire shooting schedule had to be drawn up so he was given days off during test matches.

3 Shy star, Warren Beatty will only sign a movie contract if it guarantees that he won't be filmed without a shirt, while Sylvester Stallone only allows himself to be shot in profile if it is from his good side – whichever side that is.

4 Roger Moore may have been licensed to kill when he played James Bond but he was also licensed to smoke. All his contracts guarantee him an unlimited supply of hand-rolled Cuban cigars.

Hollywood horror

After being mauled by a marauding movie mogul or signing a crazy contract, it's not surprising that some people have found the Hollywood dream turning into a nightmare. This is what some movie people have said about the horror of Hollywood.

IN HOLLYWOOD, BRIDES KEEP THE BOUQUETS AND THROW AWAY THE GROOM

GROUCHO MARX

IT IS A STRANGE PLACE WHEN YOU'RE IN TROUBLE; EVERY-ONE THINKS IT'S CONTAGIOUS

JUDY GARLAND

IN EUROPE AN ACTOR IS AN ARTIST. IN HOLLYWOOD, IF HE ISN'T WORKING, HE'S A BUM

ANTHONY QUINN

Hollyweird

Horror stories aren't the only tales to come out of Hollywood. There have also been some weird and whacky stories that have come from the capital of the movie making world. *Did you know...?*

1 In the early days of Hollywood, two silent movie stars – the Gish sisters – were given the chance to buy some land for $300. The sisters talked the matter over for a few hours then they went to a department store and bought a wildly fashionable dress each instead. That walk on the wild side proved expensive. The piece of land the sisters

were offered is now called the Sunset Strip and is worth hundreds of millions of dollars – a lot more than the dresses.

2 If the background in old Westerns look familiar, that's because most of them were filmed in the same area. At one stage, writers used to base their scripts around certain geographical features. This was great for the writers but not so good for the actors. The locations were so popular that heroes found themselves starring in some whacky chases as they rode after the wrong villains while heroines were threatened by several bunches of confused bad guys.

THIS GULCH AIN'T BIG ENOUGH FOR THE TWO, ER FOUR, ER THIRTY-SEVEN OF US

3 In 1994, ancient Egyptian remains were discovered in the Californian desert. The weird remains were eventually explained when archaeologists realized that they had found the remains of a set, believed to be from the black and white epic *The Ten Commandments,* buried under the sand.

The Hollywood sign is the most famous sign in the world. Like the larger than life industry it symbolises, the sign has had its own larger than life history. *Did you know...?*

The sign was put up in 1923. It originally said HOLLYWOODLAND and was an advertisement for property in the Hollywood Hills, not for movies.

The sign was lit by thousands of light bulbs and a man was employed to change any broken bulbs. He lived in a hut behind the double Ls.

In 1932, a failed actress called Peg Entwhistle committed suicide by jumping from the top of the thirteenth letter.

The 1991 movie, *The Rocketeer*, showed the last four letters being destroyed by a crashing Zeppelin but in reality, they were brought down by a landslide.

The sign was almost pulled down after the Second World War but after a real cliff-hanger, it was saved just in time and was declared a historic landmark in 1973. Five years later, the sign was replaced with new letters at a cost of over $243,000 and the old letters were cut up into small pieces of scrap metal which were then sold off at $29.95.

MOVIE MAGIC

Effects wizards are always dreaming up new ways of fooling audiences into believing what they are seeing. They could probably turn your headmaster into Hugh Grant – although maybe that would be a bit too difficult even for them. Stupendous effects can make you think you're really watching an actress flying through the air or a man change into a monster. Try the:

MOVIE BUFF-BUSTER QUIZ NO. 7

and see if you know just how special some effects are?

1 When Humphrey Bogart played against Ingrid Bergman in the 1942 film, *Casablanca*, he looks meaningfully into her eyes. But off screen, Bogart was only five foot four inches tall – five inches shorter than Ingrid Bergman. How did the movie makers make the stars appear to be the same height? Did they:

a ask Ingrid Bergman to kneel down during shooting
b strap five inch wooden platforms to Bogart's shoes
c use trick photography throughout the movie

2 During the filming of *Robin Hood: Prince of Thieves* in 1991, it was rumoured that Kevin Costner used a body double. Which part of his

body was the double allegedly used for. Was it:
a his right hand
b his chest
c his bottom

3 Clark Gable starred in *Gone with the Wind* and was such a big star that he was known as The King of Hollywood. "The King" was a famous sex symbol but something about him was false. Was it:
a his hair – he wore a wig
b his left leg – it was wooden
c his teeth – he wore dentures

4 In the western, *Sitting Bull*, both the Indians and the US Cavalry were played by...?
a Mexicans
b women
c small people

5 In the 1987 movie, *Superman IV*, the man of steel's home town of Metropolis was actually filmed in...
a Paris
b Milton Keynes
c New York

6 Which of the following action stars has actually been credited for doing his own stunts?
a Mel Gibson
b Roger Moore
c Errol Flynn

7 In the 1995 hit movie, *Babe,* how many piglets were filmed in the starring role.

a one
b eighty-five
c forty-eight

AND THIS LITTLE PIGGY PLAYED BABE, AND THIS LITTLE PIGGY PLAYED BABE, AND THIS LITTLE PIGGY...

8 The star of the 1996 film, *Dragonheart*, was a dragon called Draco. As well as having Sean Connery's voice, the ability to breathe fire and swim underwater, there was something extra special about Draco. Was it:

a Draco was the largest animatronic model ever made

b Draco was a virtual reality creation

c Draco was played by a horse wearing a dragon costume

Answers

1-b Humphrey Bogart wasn't the only male star with this problem. Alan Ladd's 1957 film *Boy on a Dolphin* could have been renamed *Ladd on a Box* because the star had to stand on a box when acting out love scenes with Sophia Loren.

2-c Shy stars often employ body doubles for saucy scenes.

3-c Vivien Leigh hated kissing Clark Gable when they were making *Gone with the Wind*. She complained that his dentures smelt.

4-a To make sure that the movie didn't go west at the box office, the director used lots of long shots to disguise the actors' identities.

5-b Movie makers often cheat backgrounds. One film that was set in London was actually filmed in Paris. For scenes in the 1996 Bond movie *Goldeneye*, St Petersburg was built on a film set in Watford.

6-a Mel Gibson appears twice on the credit list of the 1985 film *Mad Max Beyond Thunderdrome*, once as the leading man, once as a stunt man.

7-c The film makers used so many different piglets because the animal actors grew so quickly – not because they were worried about ham acting.

8-b Draco was added to the film by computer graphic whizzkids. During filming, the dragon's part was played by three tennis balls tied to a stick.

Real reels

Very occasionally, events on screen look so real because they were real. *Did you know...?*

1 If the sinking of the fishing boat, *The Orca*, during the 1975 movie *Jaws* looks so realistic, that's because it actually happened. When the scene was being filmed the model shark accidentally rammed the boat, taking a great bite out of it. As the boat began to sink, the camera crew abandoned ship and their camera.

The waterlogged crew were quickly rescued but the camera had disappeared overboard. Divers were hired and they eventually brought it back up to the surface. To everyone's surprise, the film inside was found to be perfect and the sinking sequence was used in the completed film.

2 In the 1962 biblical epic, *Barabbas,* special effects wizards found their skills eclipsed by real life – literally. At a particularly dramatic moment in the film, an eclipse is seen on screen and it is not a piece of movie magic. The director learned that an actual eclipse was due to take place close to where he was shooting. He hurriedly packed his cast and crew off to film the actual event and included the footage in the movie.

Film food

Movie magic isn't all about crazy car chases and stupendous stunts. When it comes to food, movie makers have thought up some really rotten recipes. Tasting this sort of film food would have a very special effect on you. If you tried any of these, you'd never complain about Aunt Gladys' sponge cake again – but then you probably wouldn't be doing any *complaining* ever again.

GROOVY MOVIE MAGIC MAG!

Rotten rain recipe

You will need a large amount of milk. Pour it into a container of water and mix well. Scatter the rotten result over the set to produce raindrops that will show up on film.

Sick-making snow

I FEEL SICK!

Take a large bowl of cornflakes. Add bleach to turn them white. Sprinkle over with a good helping of salt to give it a lovely crispy sparkle.

Splatter sauce

Pour out a large measure of chocolate sauce then dilute with water to achieve a rotten runny consistency. This recipe is best served by splattering over actors and walls for revoltingly realistic red blood effect.

Pavement pizza (or, green gloop)

Purchase or cook up a large amount of green pea soup. Add diced carrot and allow to cool. For best results, throw up large portions on set to create vile vomit.

Mucky mulch

Buy several packets of biscuits. Do not eat them. Instead, crush contents in a large container. Dilute the biscuit mulch with water to suit required recipe. If quicksand is required, add less water. Pour in more water to create slime.

Monstrous make-up

Are you fed up with seeing the same old face and the same old clothes every day? Does that face look tired and worn out? Are those clothes fit for the jumble sale? If the answer to these questions is yes, then it's time to treat your teacher to a monstrous movie make-over. Follow our top tips for a tip-top transformation.

Prepare yourself well in advance. Make sure you have plenty of spare items and that they are all within easy reach. Most importantly, don't be afraid to experiment. Simply blindfold your teacher and tie him or her tightly to a chair, all the time talking reassuringly. Remember – it's a treat that they deserve.

Hair scare

You will need a yak. If you can't get one of these at short notice, try a joke shop. Yak's hair is used to make scary hair like coarse beards and sideburns – false yak's hair is sold, too. Simply trim your yak's hair to the required shape and apply to face.

Lumps and bumps

You will need a cereal packet. Extract a few rice crispies and stick to skin to create excellent warts and other lumps and bumps. Why not add a yak's hair to a rice crispie for a revoltingly real wart?

Nail polish

Do not use nail polish. Instead, take a tin of shoe

polish and apply liberally to create dirty nails. Can also be applied to hair and face.

Monstrous menu

Mix up flour and water and mould onto skin to make hideous growths and lumps. Add different food colourings for blood, gangrene or oozing pus.

Fearsome Frankenstein

The make-up artist who created Frankenstein's monster read that the ancient Egyptians used to bind criminals hand and foot and then bury them alive. The result of this awesomely awful practice was that the corpse's arms and leg stretched and swelled up. As Frankenstein's monster was made from the bodies of executed criminals, he was made up with this look. To achieve the same look with your victim, simply shorten the sleeves and trousers with a pair of scissors.

Well done, you've done your first monstrous make-over. To finish the procedure, slowly untie your teacher from the chair, point him towards the mirror ... and run like crazy!

Surprising sounds

It's not just your eyes that are fooled by movie magic. Cinema sounds are produced in some surprisingly whacky ways. Keep your ears peeled while you match the cinema sound with the action that makes it in our:

a a raging inferno
b a flock of birds
c squeal of car tyres
d horse's hooves
e a smack on the jaw
f cutting off a limb
g squashing an insect
h a waterfall effect

1 crunching potato crisps
2 crumpling a thin piece of paper
3 a slap on the forearm
4 spraying water against a tin advertising board
5 banging coconut shells together
6 shaking leather gloves
7 sawing a cabbage in half
8 rubbing a hot water bottle against a piece of wood

Answers
a-2, b-6, c-8, d-5, e-3, f-7, g-1, h-4.

Special effects

Movie magic isn't just about special effects tricks on screen. Have you noticed how movies affect your family? Does your gran cry at soppy bits? Have you ever seen your dad hiding behind a cushion at a scary scene? Ever since an early movie of a train stopping at a station sent films fans running from the cinema, films have had some very special effects on audiences. *Did you know...?*

1 Movies have delayed battles. In 1914, the general of a group of Mexican bandits, Pancho Villa, delayed his attack on a city while he waited for a cameraman to record the battle. He had earlier signed a contract with the Mutual Film Corporation giving them exclusive rights to film his battles. To ensure that his military successes were captured on film, Villa promised the cameramen that he would only attack during daylight hours at times that were convenient for the cameras.

2 Going to the movies in the 1930s was good for your appetite. In 1934, movie star Mae West received a public thank you message from the Kansas Restaurant Association. The movie star's voluptuous shape had stopped the trend for thin figures. As film fans forgot about dieting, restaurant owners received big profits.

3 Censors* weren't the only people to get hot under the collar when soppy bits were shown on screen. During a sloppy snogging scene between Gary Cooper and Ingrid Bergman in the 1943 film *For Whom the Bell Tolls*, a reporter took the temperature in the cinema and discovered that it went up several degrees every time the scene was shown.

4 Alfred Hitchcock's 1960 film *Psycho* contains a terrifying murder scene that takes place in a shower. As well as terrifying the audience, the movie also terrified shower salesmen. After the film was released, the sales of showers plummeted.

5 The groovy gadgets shown in James Bond movies had an extraordinary effect on the KGB. Russian spy masters were convinced that the gadgets used in the movies were based on actual weapons and they set up four new divisions to try to copy the devices that 007 demonstrated in his movies.

*Censors arrived just after pictures started moving and they have one of the strangest jobs going. They need sharp eyes and even sharper scissors. Censors watch films before anyone else and decide which bits no one else should see. Normally, they're on the look-out for naughty bits or any gruesome gore. If they see a sequence that they think will put the wrong idea into people's heads then they cut it – but they manage to watch the same sequence without being affected at all. Strange indeed!

6 Movies have even moved a killer whale. Three years after escaping to freedom in the 1993 film, *Free Willy*, Keiko the killer whale was being air-lifted towards the ocean. After film fans learnt that Keiko was not having a whale of a time in his cramped tank in a Mexico City Amusement Park, they raised the money to help air-lift him to a larger pool before being released in the sea.

I'D LIKE TO THANK ALL MY FANS FOR PUTTING ME WHERE I AM TODAY...

GROOVY MOVIE MAKING

What do you think would be the grooviest way to make a movie? Watching your dad's camcorder catastrophes gives you a good idea of just how difficult it can be. With parents in charge, you never know if you're going to end up with a comedy, a horror film or a disaster movie. If you've ever tried movie-making yourself, you'll know that the trick is to keep things simple. You don't want to complicate things by asking grown-ups along, all you need do is take some friends and equipment to a suitable-looking location. That's all the early film makers did.

BUT THINGS DIDN'T STAY THAT WAY FOR LONG.
SOON FILMS GOT BIGGER ...

...AND BIGGER ...

...AND BIGGER...

... UNTIL MOVIES HAD CASTS OF THOUSANDS (AND COSTS OF MILLIONS)

Dynamic directors

Directing is the perfect job for people who like bossing other people about – so maybe your big brother might get a job after all. Nowadays, directors like George Lucas and Steven Spielberg are behind-the-scenes stars, but in the early days, the men who said "action" were not men of action and film crews thought up a new description of them – the fellows who can't do anything else.

That name didn't stick for very long. In the 1920s, one director might have been called the fellow who *wouldn't* do anything else. Cecil B. DeMille was famous for employing casts of thousands on his films and he also created a couple of unique jobs for the crew behind the camera.

DeMille concentrated on his movies so much that he didn't want to be bothered with thinking about unimportant things – such as sitting down or picking things up. As a result, he employed one person to carry his director's chair and another one to carry his megaphone. Both people had to stay alert on the job – not only would the director be too busy directing to warn them that he was about to sit down or drop his megaphone but he also carried a riding crop!

Dynamic director

Charlie Chaplin could have been called the fellow who wanted to do *everything* else. He was so dynamic that he didn't stop at directing movies – he wanted the credit for everything.

Directed by
Charlie Chaplin

Written by
Charlie Chaplin

Music composed by
Charlie Chaplin

Starring
Charlie Chaplin

With so many jobs to do, it's just as well that he was a fast worker. When he was still an unknown, Chaplin even designed his own costume. He was standing by a film set when his boss turned to him, saying, "We need some gags. Put on a comedy make-up. Anything will do."

With hardly any time to think, Chaplin ran into the nearest changing room which he shared with some other comedians and began rooting through their clothes. He grabbed some trousers belonging to Fatty Arbuckle and his father-in-law's bowler hat. Next, he put on Chester Conklin's coat and a pair of size 14 shoes that were so big that he had to wear them on the wrong feet to keep them on. Finally, he picked up a pair of scissors and trimmed some crepe hair to use as a moustache. Chaplin added his own cane and reappeared as the little tramp. His crazy costume change worked and made Chaplin into a huge star.

THAT MOUSTACHE IS CREPE

I KNOW, BUT IT'S MADE ME A STAR!

Behind the scenes stars

As soon as directors became the stars of the off-screen show, they began dressing the part.

Megaphone – for shouting cut, take one, take two and take that!

Riding crop – for cutting awful actors down to size

Riding breeches – to prove that they are at the reins

Being in the limelight off-screen wasn't enough for the English director, Alfred Hitchcock. He wasn't satisfied with his starring role behind the scenes so he cast himself in small parts in almost every film he directed, and it became a game with film-goers to spot his brief appearance.

Movie maestro

Hitchcock was a heavyweight of the movie world but even he was over-shadowed by awesome Orson Welles (1915–1985). You may not hear much about him now but he was one of the most talented movie makers ever.

Awesome Orson directed and starred in the 1941 film, *Citizen Kane*, which is possibly the grooviest movie ever made. This sounds like a good thing, but unfortunately, Orson was only in his twenties when he shot the movie. This proved to be a bad thing. After all, what do you with the rest of your life when you've already made the best movie of all time?

IT'S DOWNHILL ALL THE WAY FROM HERE!

ROSEBUD

The multi-talented movie maestro continued making movies but he was constantly distracted by other interests. He turned off his camera and turned his hand to painting and magic tricks. Eventually, the funds for his film projects began to dry up and with his budgets sawn in half, Orson needed all his magic skills to pull extra money out of the hat.

THE MIGHTY ORSINO'S
AMAZING MAGIC SHOW

PRESENTS

INCREDIBLE IMPROVISATION TRICK

When the budget for his 1951 film version of *Othello* couldn't cover costumes, Orson improvised and set the scene in a steambath – where costumes weren't needed.

THE FILM FUNDING FINALE

If all his other tricks failed, Orson threw himself on the mercy of movie makers – preferably in public places. When one of his movies had run out of money, he arrived at a hotel where movie mogul Darryl Zanuck was staying and refused to leave until Zanuck met him. When Zanuck did appear, Orson flung himself onto his knees saying, "You're the only one in the world who can save me!"

In front of so many people, the embarrassed movie mogul had no choice. He ended the scene and gave Orson the money he needed to complete his film.

Diabolical directors

If you think your teachers are tough, wait and see what some directors have done to their actors. They have used some terrible tricks to make sure that they get their shots.

1 Dastardly director Henry Lehrman was known as "Suicide" Lehrman by the people unlucky enough to be directed by him and it is easy to see why. In one early film, he let a lion loose on set without warning the cast. As the terrified actors fought to escape, the director filmed them.

127

2 When an alien bursts out of John Hurt's stomach during the 1979 film *Alien,* the looks of horror and surprise on the other actors' faces are real. The director had "forgotten" to tell them what was going to happen in the scene.

3 Alfred Hitchcock was famous for his films and for treating stars badly. Actress Tippi Hedren was almost "tippi-ed" over the edge after working on the 1963 film, *The Birds.* For one sequence, Hitchcock insisted that real birds should be used to attack his leading lady and one hungry seagull almost pecked out one of her eyes. After a week's filming, she had a nervous breakdown. Her recovery wasn't helped when Hitchcock gave her daughter, Melanie Griffith, a beautiful replica doll of her mother – in a coffin.

4 But without doubt, the award for the most diabolical director must go to John Ford. He decided that for his 1937 film *Hurricane,* the unfortunate leading man would have to do everything in the script – for real

The dictator, er director, chose a stand-in called Jon Hall to play the lead as no established actor would have anything to do with the movie. In blazing heat, Jon Hall was forced to carry a huge bag of stones then he had to dive from the top of a ship's mast before fighting a shark – a real one. Live ammunition was fired at him in the prison escape scene and he was actually horsewhipped until he bled. The cruellest cuts of all came when the film was shown to the censors. They demanded so many changes that the finished film contained nothing that couldn't have been conveyed with sound effects or make up.

Dithering directors

An indecisive director can be even more dreadful. In 1947, Billy Wilder led his set decorators a merry dance in *The Emperor Waltz*. When he arrived on location in a Canadian National Park, the director decided that some things were wrong and it took some time to get things right.

Take 1: Wilder decided that he didn't like the pine trees or their position.

Take 2: He shipped in trees from California and planted them where he wanted them.

Take 3: Wilder decided he wanted the scene sprinkled with daisies so he imported 4,000 of them.

Take 4: He then decided that he didn't like the colour of the flowers so he had them all sprayed blue.

Take 5: He wasn't sure about the colour of the roads either. They were painted ochre.

Take 6: Finally, he decided that the nearby lake was missing something – an island. He directed that an island should be built and then planted with flowers.

Just when he had driven the crew wild, the director decided he was happy with the location – and this time he didn't change his mind.

Directing disaster

When Billy Wilder eventually made up his mind he directed groovy movies, but not all directors were so excellent. If you're worried that you might not be quite as good as some of the great directors, there's no need to give up. Compared to the films of Ed Wood Junior, the films you direct will look brilliant.

Ed Wood Junior is now well-known as the worst director ever. He was so enthusiastic about finishing the movies he made that he never bothered to reshoot scenes – even if an actor had muffed their lines or bumped into a piece of furniture.

His favourite actors included a drug-addict and a bald, 400 lb Swedish wrestler. When the star of one of his movies died after a few days' filming, the ingenious director substituted a stand-in to play the part. The fact that the new actor was over a foot shorter and looked nothing like original star didn't seem to bother Ed Wood one bit.

Film family tree

Directors are still the star players behind the camera but they are given plenty of support by whole teams of specialist movie makers. However, even though movie makers are on the same team, it doesn't guarantee that they are all on the same side.

Gaffer – no, I don't make gaffes. I'm the chief electrician and sparks fly if people get on the wrong side of me.

Best boy – well spotted, you don't have to be a boy to the best boy. I'm the gaffer's assistant.

Boom operator – if I made a mistake, it would leave you speechless. I operate the microphone on set.

Cinematographer – you'd score a few own goals if you didn't take care of me. I'm responsible for the whole look of the film, choosing cameras, lenses, lighting and composition.

First assistant cameraman – I lend a hand or hand a lens to the cinematographer.

Second assistant cameraman – I've got the most famous job of all. As well as loading the camera, I also operate the clapperboard.

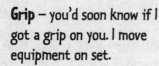

Key grip – I don't have anything to do with keys, I move the camera.

Grip – you'd soon know if I got a grip on you. I move equipment on set.

Continuity person – are you sure you were wearing that tie in the last scene? I check that visual details don't change between takes.

Location manager – when it comes to scouting around, I'm the person you want on your side. I'm in charge of finding movie locations.

First assistant director – I don't direct the movie but I do direct the running of the set.

Odd job

Have you got any special skills or party tricks that amaze and amuse your friends? Don't listen to anyone telling you that there's no point learning to unicycle while balancing a blancmange on your head. If you can do something extraordinary – and the more extraordinary the better – there's always the chance that movie makers might want you. In the 1930s, Hollywood movie makers needed someone to do one of the oddest jobs ever.

Eventually, the vacancy was filled by David Kashner who had learnt his art when he was a sheep herder in Poland. Kashner proved himself to be the whipping crème de la crème. He could crack a whip to land without any force and was so accurate that in the 1940 film, *Road to Singapore*, he whipped a rose from between the lips of the movie's star.

Although he was a crack shot, sometimes even Kashner mis-timed or mis-directed his whip but this didn't put movie extras off. In fact, they queued up to work with Kashner, hoping that he would get it wrong. On the few occasions that Kashner lashed an extra by mistake, the studio chiefs would have a quick whip round and come up with large amounts of money as compensation.

I GOT LASHINGS OF LOOT!

$

Filming a groovy movie

With so many people involved, filming a movie can be dreadfully difficult, but before you can even think about picking up a camera and hiring a crew, there are lots of obstacles to overcome. Making a movie is like running an assault course. Do you think you would reach the finish?

Obstacle 1 – The Writer's Block

Writing a script on your own can be difficult, but writing a script with someone else can be murder. In the 1940s, two writers were locked in a room together to finish a script. They got on each other's nerves so much that they made lists of the other's bad habits.

One of the writers hated his collaborator's habit of smoking a pipe. He claimed that he had to go to the bathroom frequently, just to escape from him.

The other writer found his companion even more unbearable. He complained that his co-writer wore a hat, took frequent phone calls and waved a cane around the room.

Amazingly, the two writers finished the script without killing each other. They produced the classic

136

1944 film, *Double Indemnity*, which was full of people double-crossing and murdering each other. There's no prizes for guessing where they got their inspiration from.

Obstacle 2 – Money muddles

Raising money to make a movie is even more difficult than getting a pocket money raise from your mum. To get around miserly money men, movie producers have come up with some whacky ways of coining in film funds:

1 Michael Moore raised money for his 1990 documentary film, *Roger and Me*, by running bingo games. He also collected empty soda bottles then claimed the deposit on them.

2 Two French producers raised the money for their 1987 movie, *Diary of a Madman*, by selling tickets a long way in advance. Six months before it was due to be released, they had managed to sell over 300,000 tickets.

3 One movie maker raised money by doing his own stand-up show while another simply decided to sit on street corners and beg for money from passers-by.

Obstacle 3 – Casting chaos

The amount of money you've raised will decide the sort of film you're going to make and the sort of cast you can have.

"A" movie

This is the big time. With over forty million dollars you can have big name directors, big effects and big stars. But, be warned, stars don't come cheap and they don't come on their own. During one movie, Eddie Murphy brought along two drivers, a personal trainer, a valet, five assistants and his brother. On one occasion, he treated them all to a breakfast that cost $235.33 then billed the movie makers for it.

"B" movie

Money's a lot tighter now. Star quality can be found cheaply but only if you cast groovy stars before they've become famous. Sylvester Stallone's fee for his first movie was twenty-five T-shirts while Jack Nicholson wasn't paid at all for his first screen appearance.

British movie

It's hard to get any big names for this one. You'll probably have to make do with "thingummy who was in whatsit on the telly". Your best bet may be to try some awesome animation. Wallace and Gromit began their grand day out as part of their creator's final college project before winning two Oscars. (Nick Park – see Awesome Animation p. 86).

Home movie

Borrow a camera and invite your friends round for filming. When it comes to effects, you'll need to be inventive. One movie maker's budget was so tiny that he used a cocktail shaker as a space ship in his movie!

Obstacle 4 – Preparation

Preparation is vital to movie success but sometimes it can go a bit far. As part of his preparation for the 1917 movie, *Cleopatra*, Cecil B. DeMille spent

$100,000 researching the colour of the Egyptian pyramids so that his sets would be absolutely authentic. Eventually he was told that they were sandy brown – an answer which anyone could have told him for free.

Obstacle 5 – The water jump

Warning: water-based movies can seriously damage your wealth. *Waterworld* was almost swamped by its $120 million budget in 1995, the $90 million dollar *Cut-throat Island* went to a watery grave in 1996 and *Raise the Titanic* was such a titanic flop in 1980 that its producer said that it would have been cheaper to sink the Atlantic.

The finishing line?

Congratulations, you've reached the finishing line! You've produced a script, raised some money and are prepared to begin filming, but it's too soon to think about jumping for joy or doing a lap of honour. Once you arrive on set, your troubles may only just be starting. One war film called *Apocalypse Now* turned into a behind-the-scenes horror movie. Just about everything that could go wrong, did go wrong:

Take 1. The leading man had a heart attack.

Take 2. Marlon Brando, one of the stars, arrived on set without having read the script.

Take 3. Helicopters loaned from the Philippines Government never arrived – they were being used to put down a revolution.

Take 4. The sets were destroyed by a typhoon.

Take 5. The director rewrote the script every evening after filming.

Take 6. The crew began drinking and taking drugs.

Amazingly, the movie did actually get made in 1979. A few years later *Hearts of Darkness*, a movie about making the movie, was also released.

Cruel cuts

You've survived shooting but can your groovy movie cope with cruel cuts? Scissor-happy censors are always trying to chop bits out of films. If your mum and big sister love snogs and soppy bits, they wouldn't have liked film censors in the 1920s and 1930s. The censors came up with some whacky ways to stop movie makers who might be tempted to film some sloppy snogs or even show some naughty bits. They decided it would be a good thing to introduce a few rules:

1 A time limit for snogs. Kisses were only allowed to last for five sloppy seconds.

141

2 Movie stars had to keep both feet on the ground when they snogged.

3 Married couples always had to have separate beds.

4 Any footage that broke the rules had to be cut.

5 Er, that's it. No more rules.

Censor's snips

It hasn't just been snogs and soppy bits that have got the censors hot under the collar. Which of the following do you think have been cruelly cut from films? Here comes:

1 A piece of Stilton cheese

2 A woman's elbow

3 Mickey Mouse

4 A cartoon cow's udder

5 The screech of car tyres

6 Kevin Costner's first starring role

Answer
All of them!

1 The first demand for a cruel cut was in 1898 when a scientist released a film that showed the activity of bacteria in a piece of Stilton.

2 The offending elbow belonged to Sylvia Sidney and was exposed in the 1932 film version of *Madame Butterfly*. When the movie was shown in Japan, the entire scene was given the elbow by the censors.

3 Mickey Mouse was banned in Romania in 1935 because the authorities thought he would frighten children.

4 Clarabelle the cartoon cow's udder was considered so "udderly" naughty in the 1930s that the censors ordered that she must wear a skirt in all future appearances.

5 In one Hollywood movie that was made during the Second World War, the screech of car tyres was cut for being "contrary to the rubber conservation programme".

6 Kevin Costner got his big break in the 1980s film *The Big Chill* when he landed a major role. Unfortunately his entire role ended up on the cutting room floor. He wasn't cruelly cut because of any awful acting – the film was just too long.

Kind cuts

Censors aren't the only people who cut movies. Editing sounds like a simple job and cutting clips out of film isn't too hard – it's putting the film back together without showing the joins that is the real skill. Directors keep their editors busy because they shoot more film than they need. It can take months to edit a feature film but very occasionally the editor should have spent just a few more minutes on the job. A few kind cuts would have kept some groovy goofs off the big screen. If you keep your eyes peeled you might spot them:

1 In Hitchcock's 1954 thriller, *Rear Window*, the leading man breaks his leg but he doesn't seem to know which one. The plaster cast swaps legs throughout the movie.

2 At the end of the 1985 movie, *The Goonies*, one of the gang says that the best part of the adventure was fighting with the octopus. Unfortunately, that scene had been cut out of the movie and was not in the finished version.

3 When Indiana Jones sets off across the Atlantic on his last crusade, the date is 1938 but when he is waiting in the departure lounge, two passengers can be seen reading German newspapers – from 1918.

Film failures

Triumph or turkey?
At last, your groovy movie is ready to be released. It's cleared the movie making obstacle course and

survived cruel cuts but will it survive at the box office? No one knows the recipe for a box office smash. Which of the two films below do you think would be a triumph, which one would be a turkey?

FILM 1 – A RECIPE FOR SUCCESS?

Step 1. Take two big box office stars – Dustin Hoffman and Warren Beatty.

Step 2. Mix in with star writer/director, Elaine May.

Step 3. Add a budget of $50 million dollars.

Step 4. Garnish with a large and expensive advertising campaign, supported by Columbia Studios.

Step 5. Place in cinemas then sit back and wait for profits to rise.

FILM 2 – A PERFECT TURKEY?

Step 1. Take an unknown British actor
Step 2. Add a writer with some television comedy success.
Step 3. Sprinkle over with a scant budget of six million dollars.
Step 4. Run a short advertising campaign and distribute the film through various small companies.
Step 5. Keep fingers crossed as you book a limited release in the USA.

Answer

Film 1 is *Ishtar* which became one of biggest film turkeys when it was released in 1987.

Film 2 is *Four Weddings and a Funeral*. This became one of the most successful British movies ever when it hit the cinema screens in 1994.

Precious publicity

Before your movie is ready to hit the cinemas, there's last one thing to organize. Publicity is precious for movie makers and publicity people are always trying to come up with bigger and better ways to make sure that audiences roll up to see their movie. Can you think of any amazing antics that should be in the top ten stupendous publicity stunts?

[10]

Coming in at number ten is the old tie trick. Before the First World War, cinema owners handed out huge, hideously-coloured ties to people queuing up outside the cinema and promised a free seat to anyone brave enough to wear them throughout the movie.

[9]

And for all you publicity-pickers, number nine is a great ruse cooked up to publicize the 1988 film, *Babette's Feast*. The last part of this film features a wonderful, mouth-watering meal. When the filmed opened in New York, film fans were able to feast their eyes on the food on screen then feast on the same meal at a nearby restaurant.

A non-mover at number eight is the beastly beard stunt. Growing a beard might not seem such a stupendous stunt but when screen idol, Rudolph Valentino, stopped shaving, a storm of outrage rose from fans and barbers. A public shaving ceremony followed a few months later.

Flying in at number seven is the publicity saying, the bigger the star, the bigger the stunt. In 1993, a 75 foot balloon with Arnold Schwarzenegger's picture on it was flown above Times Square in New York to advertise one of his movies.

Straight in at number six is the super slogan. The publicity department at 20th Century Fox weren't counting their chickens when they released the epic 1954 movie, *The Egyptian* — they were counting something else. The film's super slogan claimed that the film featured 10,965 pyramids, 5,337 dancing bulls, one million swaying bulrushes and 802 sacred bulls.

Dastardly director, Alfred Hitchcock, enters the top ten at five with the only stupendous stunt that was legally enforceable. When his film *Psycho* was released in 1960, no one was allowed into the cinema if the film had already started.

Holding firm at number four is the Lawrence Lie. When producer Carl Laemmle decided that he wanted to make a star out of a young actress called Florence Lawrence, he decided to lie. In 1910, he planted a false story in a newspaper that Lawrence had been tragically killed in a car crash. Once the public's appetite had been whetted, the producer then placed an advert in the same paper revealing that the star was alive and was about to appear in a new film.

Standing still at three is a splendid stunt that cost the publicity team more than they bargained for. To publicize a 1932 movie called *The Man I Killed*, an unemployed man was hired to be buried in a grave for twenty four hours. The man was buried during the day but that night a severe storm destroyed the grave marker. The panicking publicists had to pay for a team of over 30 men to

ER... HELLO? I'M READY FOR MY CLOSE-UP NOW...

dig up the area and when they eventually found the man, he immediately demanded overtime money.

2

At number two, we've got a publicity ruse that ran for over two years. That was the time it took to screen test over two thousand hopefuls in a well-publicized attempt to find the female lead for *Gone with the Wind*. Vivien Leigh eventually got the part but it was such a difficult choice that the film had begun shooting before she was picked.

1

Occupying the top slot is the longest-running movie stunt. On 18 May 1927, film star Norma Talmadge is supposed to have stepped in some wet cement outside Grauman's Chinese Theatre by mistake. The concrete set preserving the star's footprints for posterity and this "accident" started the stunt which continues to this day.

Forgotten films

There are some films that even the most stupendous stunts can't save. Some of the grooviest movie stars have appeared in films they would rather forget.:

MOVIE BUFF-BUSTER

QUIZ | NO. 10

Do you know which big names appeared in the following turkeys?

1 *Earth Girls are Easy*
2 *Paint Your Wagon*
3 *Hudson Hawk*
4 *Grease 2*
5 *Hercules in New York*

a Bruce Willis
b Michelle Pfeiffer
c Arnold Schwarzenegger
d Jim Carey
e Clint Eastwood

Answers

1-d Jim Carey's early appearance in this film was as a fur-covered alien.

2-e Clint as you've never seen or heard him before in this musical Western.

3-a The biggest-ever movie flop. It cost $65 million and took back less than $9 million.

4-b The reason why there was never a *Grease 3*.

5-c Arnold in a toga and sandals in modern-day New York!

GROOVY MOVIE GOING

Going to the movies is so groovy that even your mum and dad have probably done it. Of course, movies have changed a lot since their days – now they're in colour and have got sound – and so have cinemas.

If your parents are always going on about what things were like in the good old days, why not see how much they *really* know about the early days of groovy movie-going? Dim the lights, pass the popcorn and watch how they get on with:

MOVIE BUFF-BUSTER

QUIZ NO.11

1 In 1898, when the miracle of moving pictures was sweeping through the world, where was the best place to catch a movie?
   a A music hall.
   b A shop.
   c Some nearby railway arches.

2 Early cinemas in America were called Nickelodeons. Do you know why?
   a They were built from nickel.
   b They were named after the founders of the company that owned them – Mr Nickel and Mr Odeon.
   c It cost a nickel to get into one.

MR FLEA MR PIT

151

3 Around 1905, one film company specialized in strapping cameras to the front of locomotives and filming the following railway journeys. To add to the train journey effect, Hales Tours designed a groovy gimmick. *Was it...?*

a Hales Tours cinemas were designed to look like a railway coach.

b Tickets to a Hales Tours film were stamped by an attendant in a ticket inspector's uniform.

c Staff at cinemas showing Hales Tours films were given whistles and flags to wave during the show.

4 The largest cinema ever built was opened in 1927. It cost twelve million dollars but how many film fans were needed for a full house? Was it...?

a Four thousand
b Six thousand
c Ten thousand

5 In 1933, a new kind of fabby film house was patented by Mr Richard M. Hollingshead Jnr. These cinemas were soon nicknamed "Ozoners"," Cow Pastures" and "Under the Stars Emporiums". Do you know why?

a They were built on farms

b They had retractable roofs

c They had giant screens which the audience drove to

Multiple choice answers

1 – all of these. Film fans would be better off trying any of these places than looking for a

152

cinema. Movies were so new that cinemas hadn't been built yet. Existing buildings were converted or the walls of railway arches were used to show films.

2-c The British equivalents were called Penny Gaffs for the same reason – the entrance fee was one penny. Even in those days, that wasn't very expensive which is just as well because film fans didn't get much for their money. Penny Gaffs were small, dingy places with ordinary kitchen chairs to sit on.

3-a Hale Tours cinemas had a central aisle with railway carriage seats on either side.

4-b Samuel Lionel Rothapfel called himself the world's greatest showman. He built several huge cinemas, each one bigger than the next. With typical modesty, he called the biggest one "The Roxy" after his nickname.

5-c Drive-in movies were so popular that their inventor could not enforce his patent. One American cinema owner made sure his movie house really took off by advertising a Fly-In which had spaces for twenty-five planes. New Yorkers can experience drive-in movies without driving anywhere. At one cinema, the audience sit in classic 1950s cars under a ceiling that is painted with stars to watch B movies and 1950s newsreels.

Picture palaces

You might think that multiplexes are the best thing since colour telly but they are outclassed by the funkiest film houses of them all – the picture palaces. With a name like that, you don't have to be a genius to work out what they were like. Crowds of movie goers flocked to see the exotic props, fabulous scenery and great costumes – and that was just in the cinema. Visiting a picture palace wasn't like watching a movie, it was like being in one.

If someone in the 1920s asked you if you fancied Chinese, they wouldn't have been asking you about food, they would be inviting you to the cinema. Some picture palaces were built to look like Chinese Pagodas but if that wasn't to your taste, you could try Italian or Spanish-style castles.

If the architecture was over the top, so were the descriptions of Picture Palaces. Out went "cold", "draughty" and "fleapit" to be replaced with "An Acre of Seats in a Garden of Dreams" or "The Temple of Motion Pictures".

Picture palaces were just the ticket for funky film fans but they didn't just have to watch a film when they visited one. In fact, there were so many other things to do, movie goers could easily forget why there were there.

THE PICTURE PALACE IS PROUD TO PRESENT THE BEST IN MOVIE ENTERTAINMENT

DIAL "F" FOR FREE
– E.T. could have phoned home from a picture palace as local phone calls were provided for free.

BIGFOOT
– the audience could put their best foot forward in one picture palace that housed a chiropodist.

HOT SHOTS
– if you missed your showing, you could show off your billiards or table tennis skills.

ALADINTIGHTS
– before the curtain opened on the movie, the curtains opened on ballet troupes.

THE RACKETEERS
– in the days before soundtracks, mighty wurlitzers provided the music. The organists became unlikely stars and most famous (and the most unlikely) were the three racketeering Reginalds – Dixon, Foort and Porter-Brown.

STRICTLY BALLROOM
– tap your toes to the wurlitzer then tap your toes on the dance floor.

WHO FRAMED ROGER RABBIT?
– film fans didn't just have to check out the movie, works of art were often hung on cinema walls.

BARON MUNCHAUSEN
– picture palaces didn't sell snacks, they had restaurants that served four course meals.

PEE-WEE'S BIG ADVENTURE
– use your imagination to work out which facilities this movie describes.

Ridiculous rules

There are always people who want to spoil everyone else's fun. Normally, of course, they're teachers but in the 1920s even they liked going to the movies. Instead, "polite people" decided that movie-going was too enjoyable so they dreamt up some really ridiculous rules on correct cinema conduct.

When visiting a movie theatre in a group:
DO know your exact seat.
DO NOT block the aisle while waiting to be told your seat.

When acting as host to a group visiting a movie theatre:
DO send people to their seats in the correct order.
DO NOT send ladies to their seats first then let their gentlemen escorts stumble across them.

When visiting a movie theatre with one's wife:
DO stand aside for your wife to sit down first.
DO NOT allow your wife to sit in an aisle seat.

If passing across people already seated:
DO face the screen and stay as close as possible to the backs of the facing seats.
DO NOT drag anything across the heads of those sitting in the facing seats – imagine the disastrous

consequences that such an action might have upon the hair-dressing of a lady in a row in front of you.

If forced to pass in front of someone who gets up or lets you pass:

DO employ the correct phrase such as "Thank you", "Thank you very much" or "I am sorry".

DO NOT employ the current expression "beg pardon". This is an abbreviation and is one of the phrases never spoken in polite society.

When watching a movie:

DO remain attentive and quiet.

DO NOT be so inconsiderate or impolite as to read any captions out loud.

Groovy gimmick-o-rama

Luckily, movie-goers were far too groovy to be put off by such ridiculous rules, but in the 1950s, a cure for movie madness was invented. It was called television and it was administered in long doses every evening. Things were looking bad and not just because early TVs had such poor reception. Cinema owners decided to fight back. In order to beat "the little monster in the living room", some seriously groovy gimmicks were dreamt up. Which do you think were actually tried out?

Smell-O-Vision – scents piped into the cinema via plastic tubes during films

Sensurround – soundtracks were amplified in certain scenes to cause a rumbling sensation

Odorama – audience given a scratch and sniff card with instructions on when to scratch

Waterwatch – special tanks were installed under the seats then flooded with water

Emergo – a skeleton on wires was dropped over the audience's head

3-D Vision – audience given 3-D glasses to enable them to see three dimensional effects in the film

Quakorama – seats fitted with wheels that rocked at appropriate moments during films

Terrorvision – all members of the audience issued with a life insurance policy in case anyone died of fright during the movie

Shock-O – chairs wired up to give a mild electric shock at a particular point in the movie

Illusion-O – audience given special filtered glasses to see ghosts on screen that were otherwise invisible

The Horror Horn – a horn was sounded to warn the audience of a particularly horrifying scene

Duovision – a movie was shown entirely in split-screen format

Murder Minute – a 60 second break at the climax of the film allowing the viewer to solve the mystery

EPILOGUE

Luckily, film fans managed to survive the groovy gimmicks of the 1950s and even more luckily, movies survived the invention of TV.

In just over one hundred years, movies have had some very special effects. They've got up people's noses, they've even ruined a few people's lives but they've been enjoyed by millions of film fans every day.

Of course, one of the grooviest things about movies is that they are still being made. With more films and more film fans being bitten by the movie bug, the movie world is getting bigger and groovier all the time.

If this book has helped put you in the picture then who knows, maybe one day you'll become a groovy movie maker yourself. If that happens, it'll guarantee that we can finish with a traditional Hollywood happy ending.

THE END